Wildlife Walks:
Birmingham and the Black Country

10 short walks described by
Peter Shirley

Illustrated by Julia Morland

Foreword by Chris Baines

Based on BBC Radio WM's Series
'A Breath of Fresh Air'

WAYSIDE BOOKS
CLEVEDON, AVON

Other books in the *Wildlife Walkabouts* series:
Avon and Somerset Border (ISBN 0-948264-00-4 Pbk)
South Cotswolds and North Avon (ISBN 0-948264-02-0 Pbk)
Land's End Peninsula, Cornwall (ISBN 0-948264-01-2 Pbk)
Lizard to Mid-Cornwall (ISBN 0-948264-03-9 Pbk)

These books are available in most good bookshops, especially in the areas they cover, but in case of any difficulty please contact the publishers:
Wayside Books, 3 Park Road, Clevedon, Avon BS21 7JG

British Library Cataloguing in Publication Data

Shirley, Peter
    Wildlife walkabouts : Birmingham and the Black Country.
    1. (Metropolitan County) West Midlands. Black Country. Organisms.
    I. Title
    574.9424'9

ISBN 0-948264-04-7

First published in 1988 by
Wayside Books
3 Park Road, Clevedon, Avon BS21 7JG
Telephone (0272) 874750

Text copyright © 1988 Peter Shirley
Illustrations coyright © 1988 Julia Morland
Text for section 'Keys to Identifying Wildlife' copyright © 1985 Michael Woods
Illustrations for section 'Keys to Identifying Wildlife' copyright © 1985 Julia Morland
Photographs copyright © 1988 Ralph Sandoe unless credited

Design, make-up and maps by Ralph Sandoe, Wayside Books

Wildlife Walkabouts series copy edited by Edward Sparkes, Clifton, Bristol

Typeset by Wayside Books, Clevedon, Avon BS21 7JG
Repro by Westspring Graphics, Weston-super-Mare, Avon BS23 IQF
Printed and bound by WBC Print Limited, St. Philips, Bristol BS2 0RL

*To all the members of Sandwell Valley Field Naturalists' Club
who have opened my eyes to so much*

Acknowledgements

This book would not have been possible without the help of many people. In particular I thank publisher Ralph Sandoe for the patient way he dealt with a new author, illustrator Julia Morland who has produced many fine drawings whilst coping with a new baby, Chris Baines for his Foreword, and John Pickles, Phil Horner and Tony Inchley of BBC Radio WM, who helped to make the whole thing possible. Other valuable contributions were made by Ted Sparkes, Derek Brown (Birmingham City Conservation Officer), Joy Fifer, Chris Parry, Cathy Wells and Barry Rowe of the Urban Wildlife Group, Alan Harris and Graham Perry of Saltwells Wood, and Heather While and John Price of the Woodgate Valley. Finally, thanks to my wife Dot both for her advice and her understanding.

Publisher's Note

This book is the fifth in the series entitled *Wildlife Walkabouts*. The publisher anticipates producing others covering different areas. With this in mind the publisher and author welcome any constructive criticism or praise from readers on any aspect of this publication. Please write to the publisher, or author, at Wayside Books, 3 Park Road, Clevedon, Avon BS21 7JG.

Permission to photocopy. The author and illustrator have kindly given permission for the owner of this book to obtain a single photocopy of any page or pages between 11 and 110 inclusive for personal use whilst walking the routes. If the book itself is used on the walks, a protective plastic cover, obtainable from most good booksellers and stationers, would help to keep it in good condition.

The routes of these walks, as far as could be ascertained, follow public rights of way which were in existence at the time of going to press. No responsibility can be taken by the author or the publisher for any errors in this book which may lead to action being taken against readers and users as a result of these.

CONTENTS

List of Illustrations in Text 6
Foreword by Chris Baines 7
Country Code 8
Introduction by Peter Shirley 9
The Urban Wildlife Group 10

The Walks:

    Sandwell Valley 11
    Saltwells Wood 21
    Sutton Park 31
    Plants Brook 41
    Great Barr – Urban Safari 51
    Moseley Bog 61
    Woodgate Valley 71
    Harborne Line Walkway 81
    Chasewater 91
    Galton Valley 101

Keys to Identifying Wildlife 111

    Birds 112
    Plants 115
    Ferns 116
    Trees 117
    Mammals 118
    Insects and Spiders 122

Wildlife and the Law 123
List of Organisations 124
Bibliography 125
Index 126

LIST OF ILLUSTRATIONS IN TEXT

Aeshna, brown 55
Alfalfa (Lucerne) 86
Arion slug 98

Banded snail 90
Beech 69
Beech mast 28
Bilberry 96
Bindweed 48
Bluebell 23
Bryony, white 48
Bullfinch 64
Butterwort 39

Canada goose 55
Carp 16
Chicory 54
Cinquefoil, marsh 100
Colt's-foot 64
Cowslip 79

Damselfly nymph 47
Daphnia 46
Dragonfly nymph 47

Emperor moth 40

Fieldfare 64
Fox 109
Frog, common 65

Garden spider 75
Goldeneye duck 94
Goldfinch 77
Grass snake 26
Grasshopper 104
Greater celandine 47
Greater spearwort 16
Greater stitchwort 28
Grebe, great crested 95
Gull, great black-backed 99

Hairstreak, green 27
Hairstreak, purple 20
Harvestman 85
Hawthorn 64
Heather 40
Holly 36
Holly blue 36
Honeysuckle 48
Horsetail, wood 68

Ichneumon wasp 106
Ivy 66

Kingfisher 49

Lime 54
Liverworts 38
Lucerne (alfalfa) 86

Male fern 84
Martin, house 86
Mayfly nymph 47
Merlin 44
Mink 30
Moorhen 105
Moschatel 76
Mussel, painter's 37

Newt, smooth 46
Nightshade, enchanter's 29
Nightshade, woody 56
Noctule bat 19
Nuthatch 28

Oak, holm 14
Oak, Turkey 107
Orchid, Southern marsh 45
Oyster fungus 57

Pansy, field 103

Ragged-robin 80
Red admiral 89
Roach 59
Royal fern 67
Ruddy ducks 17

Scabious, devil's-bit 34
Scabious, field 88
Scorpionfly 60
Small heath 97
Snipe 39
Southern hawker 87
Sparrowhawk 77
Speckled wood 27
Squirrel, grey 60
Stickleback, three-spined 110
Sulphur tuft 34
Sundew, round-leaved 100

Tansy 109
Teasel 77
Thrushes anvil 90
Tufted hair-grass 75

Vole, water 50

Wagtail, pied 93
Weasel 79
Woodpecker, great spotted 70
Wormwood 45

Yellow archangel 76
Yellow-wort 59

FOREWORD

To the outside world, the image of the West Midlands is one of noise and grime. Hardly the place for a 'wildlife walkabout'. In fact, the whole region is extraordinarily green and wild – a scattering of towns and villages set in a leafy landscape. Some of the urban green is captive countryside locked in by the building boom of the 19th century's Industrial Revolution and containing fragments of ancient woodland, heathland and meadow. A great deal of the land is old industrial dereliction – clay pits, coal tips, quarries and mining settlements, long since abandoned, and now carpeted with a rich tapestry of birch woodland, rosebay willowherb and bramble. This is the ideal habitat for songbirds, butterflies, and local kids, and it's so much wilder than our neat and tidy farming countryside.

Such an extensive network of green landscape would quite naturally be rich in wildlife, but the urban West Midlands has an added bonus; it is relatively free from chemical pollution – no one is spraying with farm chemicals. Most of the polluting industry has collapsed or been cleaned up, and so it is possible to see kingfishers and dragonflies, frogs and newts, in fact a whole host of wild plants and animals which have declined dramatically in the chemically-farmed countryside in recent years.

This rich wild landscape is not always easy to find; it's hidden behind the houses and factories. But, once 'shown the way', it is possible to walk for miles along the canal towpaths, the derelict railway lines and the riverside footpaths, without ever needing to cross a road, and you will never be faced with ploughed footpaths or 'Beware of the Bull' signs.

This book is a marvellous introduction to one of the best-kept secrets of the British landscape. Use it to discover the wild places of the West Midlands, and you will begin to see every other urban sprawl you pass through as the rich green tapestry of unofficial countryside it really is.

Chris Baines

COUNTRY CODE

Wherever you go:

Enjoy the countryside and respect its life and work
Guard against all risk of fire
Fasten all gates
Keep dogs under close control
Keep to public paths across farmland
Use gates and stiles to cross fences, hedges and walls
Leave livestock, crops and machinery alone
Take all litter home
Help to keep all water clean
Protect wildlife, plants and trees
Take care on roads especially when crossing
Make no unnecessary noise
Park considerately
Respect local residents

INTRODUCTION

In this book I have described ten short walks within one of the most industrialised areas of Britain. That being so it may be surprising to some of you that there is so much wildlife and attractive landscape to talk about. Come with me and discover this half-hidden world between and behind the houses and factories. We will go from secret places where a railway ran to wide open spaces once enjoyed by Henry VIII, and from ancient hedgerows to old reservoirs. All of the sites have been featured in Radio WM's series 'A Breath of Fresh Air' during the past four years. There are many more, equally rich in plants and animals, which the programme visited but which could not be included here.

I have tried to give a broad picture of the wildlife in each place. You will see many things other than those mentioned. On the other hand you may not find some of the birds, plants or animals featured. The season, the time of day, the weather, the light, your own way of approaching a place – all of these have a bearing upon what may be seen. Remember though that nature never lets us down. Wherever and whenever you visit there will always be colour, movement and sound.

Wildlife in towns and cities falls broadly into three categories. There are the things which have survived in special places whilst the town has grown around them: the rare wood horsetail in Moseley Bog and the grass snakes in Saltwells Wood, for example, whose homes have both been encapsulated by development. There are the species which find that man and his activities suit their life style very well: the frogs and newts in our garden ponds, and the house martins who find no difference between the eaves of houses and overhanging ledges on cliffs. Finally there are the travellers: birds, butterflies and other insects, which pass through on migration stopping for refreshment in our wetlands, gardens and informal open spaces. All together they form an ever-changing kaleidoscope of beauty and wonder.

The urban naturalists of today have much in common with the famous 18th-century naturalist, Gilbert White. Not for him, nor them, the rain forests of the tropics, the coral reefs in warm seas, or the tundra of the frozen north. Instead, his pleasure, as it is for them, was in the everyday contact he had with the 'citizens' of the natural world in the place where he lived. (In the case of these urban walks 'citizen' is used with its meaning of 'town dweller'.) Living all his life in the South of England, White was able to write to a friend in April 1768: 'I shall still live in hopes of seeing you at this beautiful season, when every hedge and field abounds with matter of entertainment for the curious'. In this book, as well as 'hedge and field', we have 'canal towpath and old mineral working'. I hope I have pointed the way. I know that the wildlife is there, I am sure you will find pleasure in it.

Peter Shirley
West Bromwich, West Midlands
1988

THE URBAN WILDLIFE GROUP

The Urban Wildlife Group was formed in 1980 and is the nature conservation trust for Birmingham and the Black Country. Peter Shirley, the author of this book, is its full-time Director. Believing firmly that people and wildlife can co-exist in cities to their mutual benefit, its main aims are to:

- increase awareness of the need to foster natural history in the West Midlands' conurbation
- campaign to protect existing sites of wildlife value and improve others
- promote ideas and inspiration for combining natural history and recreation in urban open spaces.
- encourage and help other similar groups in their efforts to conserve and study wildlife
- educate people to a wider understanding of the nature on their doorsteps, and to enjoy and preserve it
- tackle the practical problems of managing urban open spaces for both conservation and amenity
- positively encourage nature conservation policy and planning within local government, institutions, and private landowners
- to pursue every opportunity to create long-term job opportunities in nature conservation.

The Group is a registered charity affiliated to the Royal Society for Nature Conservation. As such it is heavily dependent upon members' subscriptions to sustain its work. Details of membership should be obtained from its office at:

> 131–133 Sherlock Street,
> Birmingham
> B5 6NB.

SANDWELL VALLEY

It is worth a pause on the wooden bridge over the pond before the uphill part of the walk begins

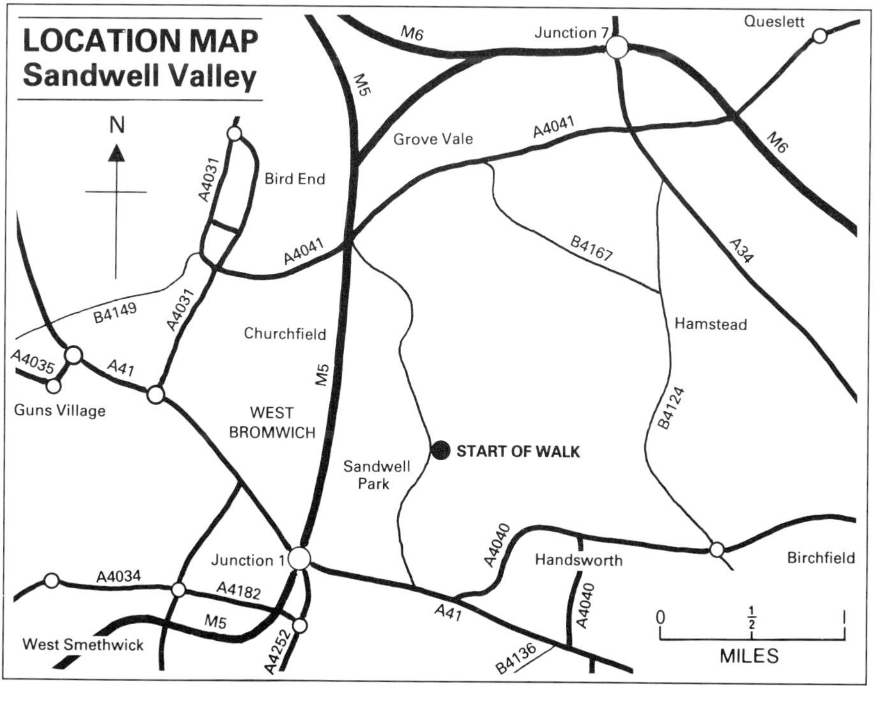

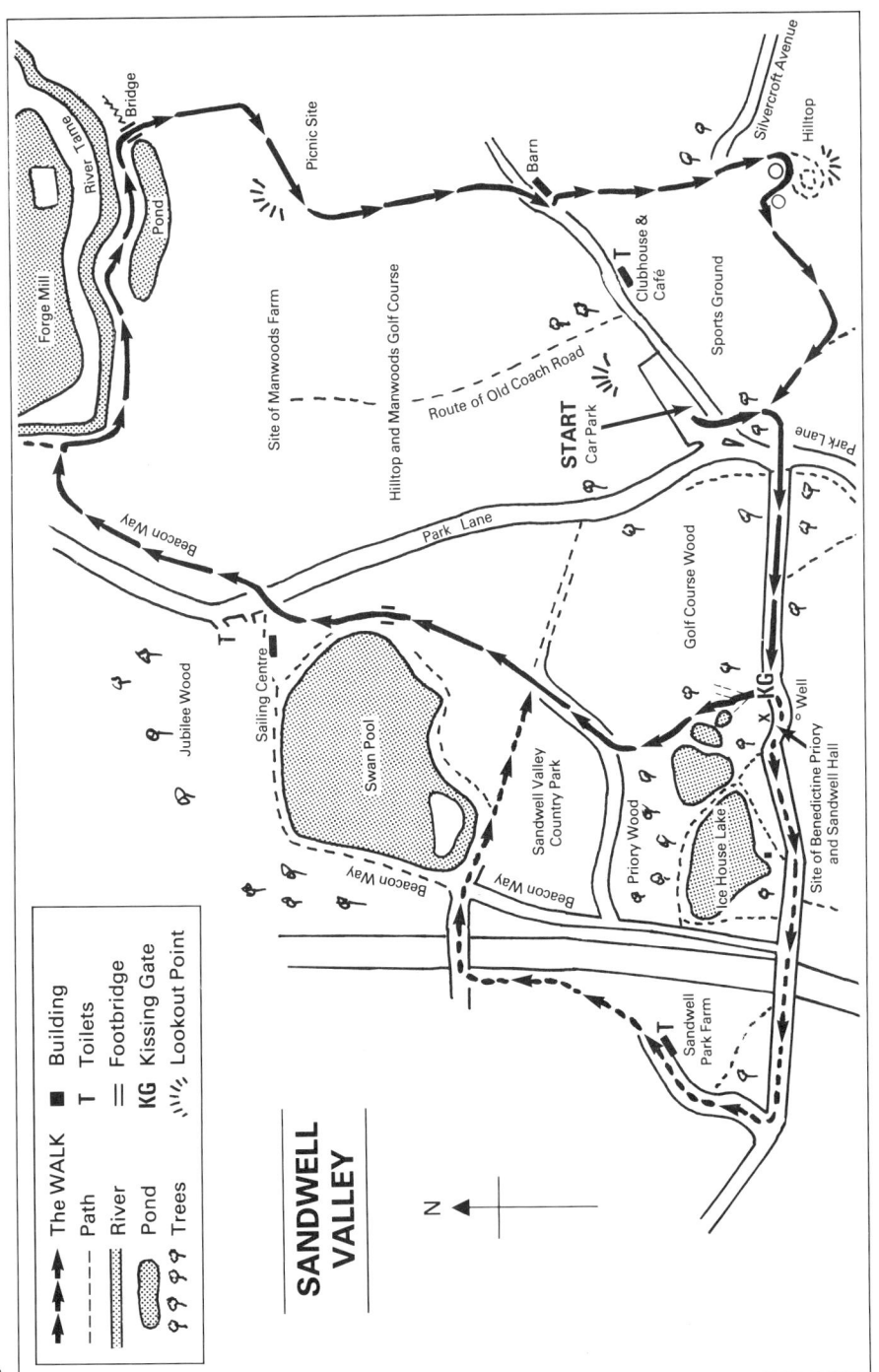

SANDWELL VALLEY

O.S. SP09 (1:25000) – 031914 Approx. 3½ miles

A walk through open land only a few miles from Birmingham city centre. Gently undulating slopes, the Birmingham skyline, and a great variety of birds, plants, animals and insects provide a fascinating walk at any time of the year. Easy walking but there can be a lot of mud in places.

The 2,500 acres of the Sandwell Valley have never been developed but they have a varied and continuous history of use. During the past 1,000 years there has been a priory here, an 18th-century stately home (complete with manicured parkland), farms on the hillsides, and mills along the river. Now a country park nestles cheek by jowl with golf courses, and modern civilisation intrudes with its railways and roads. Through all the changes the local wildlife has survived, especially in and around the quiet woods and the gentle streams and pools. Two working farms and two show farms perpetuate the rural nature of the valley. Their small fields, grazing animals and sinuous hedgerows, present a scene surprising both for its time and its place.

Park in the public car park off Park Lane at Hill Top Golf Club. Walk back towards the entrance and take the metalled path to the left through the wooded area. Turn right to cross Park Lane and enter Sandwell Valley Country Park through the gateway. Walk straight on.

As you leave the car park during an autumn afternoon the brilliant green of the 'improved' grass on the football pitches will very likely be dotted with the white and grey plumage of black-headed gulls. Little else is seen there except for these birds. The darting jabs of their red bills gives them the appearance of making urgent repairs to the fabric of the field. In reality, of course, they are snapping up the mini-beasts lurking in the turf. Their isolation emphasises their adaptability and is a pointer to their success as an urban species so far from the sea considering football pitches are recent arrivals in terms of the evolution of birds. Black-headed gulls (and a few other species) have already learned to exploit them for food and by so doing have added to their chances of surviving and breeding.

Gulls may often be seen stamping their feet on football pitches. This is not to keep warm – the vibrations stimulate earthworms to come to the surface where are easily snapped up.

The small wood between the car park and the road has virtually no undergrowth. Look how far one can see through the trees, many of which are about the same size. This is typical of heavily-used but more or less unmanaged woodland. The more sensitive members of the natural woodland community are trampled out of existence. The trees themselves do not regenerate properly and so the whole wood becomes 'even-aged'. This makes it less robust, more vulnerable to change and stress, and puts its long-term future at risk. Fortunately steps are being taken to manage the valley's woodlands in a way that should help them to flourish.

13

As the leaves fall they reveal the presence of grey squirrel dreys. They are easily distinguished from birds' nests by their size and rather untidy appearance caused by the dead leaves attached to the branches of which they are made. Dreys are roughly spherical, perhaps nearest in shape and size to a magpie's nest. The magpie's home, however, is built in early spring before there are any leaves on the twigs, the extra insulation coming from lining the nest with mud. Contrary to popular opinion squirrels do not hibernate. Their eager foraging amongst leaf litter, peek-a-boo antics whilst climbing tree trunks, and their high-speed, high-wire act through the branches overhead, enliven many a winter walk. Like foxes, they enjoy an amicable relationship with town-dwellers which is not always reflected in that of their respective country cousins.

Once over the road, the oak and birch woodland on the left contrasts with the open fields and pastures to the right. A little way ahead lies the site of a series of buildings which culminated in the building of Sandwell Hall in the early 1700s. This was the home of the Earls of Dartmouth. An avenue of sweet chestnut was planted which led to the front entrance, the last remains of which can still be seen. The few trees that are left have short thick boles and very few branches, an example being on the right of the path.

At the kissing gate on the right there is a choice of route.

Continuing straight ahead takes the walker past the archaeological excavations, over the motorway, and to valley's interpretation centre at Park Farm. The walk can be rejoined at Swan Pool by crossing the paddocks to go over the northern motorway bridge.

Alternatively go through the gate, cross the small wooden bridge, bear right and then turn left at the next path junction and left at the fork. Turn right by an old tree-stump, cross the ditch and follow the path to the left. Turn right at the main path and walk towards Swan Pool.

The excavations show the remains of Sandwell Priory which was built between 1180 and 1190. It was a Benedictine house, dedicated to Mary Magdalene. The monks farmed the area and, like so many people since, took advantage of the clear springs of pure water to build pools, theirs being used to keep a supply of fresh fish handy. Later pools were constructed for ornamental purposes and more recently to enhance the natural history interest of the valley, or for recreation. The priory was built near to a hermitage located by one particular spring known as the Holy or Sand Well. This historic site thus provided the name of the new borough created in the 1970s. It is the largest of the four 'Black Country' boroughs with a population of 300,000. After the suppression of the priory in

Holm oak

1525 (attended to by no less a person than Thomas Cromwell) a dwelling known as Priory House was occupied. The name was changed to Sandwell Hall before it was acquired by the Dartmouths who demolished it and built a new hall which stood until 1928. This church mouse would doubtless have been quite at home in the priory church writing its diary (excepting, of course, its catholic antecedents):

Here among long-discarded cassocks,
Damp stools, and half-split open cassocks,
Here where the vicar never looks
I nibble through old service books.
Lean and alone I spend my days
Behind this Church of England baize.
I share my dark forgotten room
With two oil lamps and half a broom.
The cleaner never bothers me,
So here I eat my frugal tea.
My bread is sawdust mixed with straw;
My jam is polish for the floor.

Christmas and Easter may be feasts
For congregations and for priests,
And so may Whitsun. All the same,
They do not fill my meagre frame.
For me the only feast at all
Is autumn's Harvest Festival,
When I can satisfy my want
With ears of corn around the font.

From *Diary of a Church Mouse*, a poem by John Betjeman

The farm which lies on the other side of the motorway served the estate. It is a beautiful example of a 17th-century farm, even though it was built in the early 18th century. It is very different in form to the Georgian farms of the later 1700s constructed during the enactment of the enclosures legislation. The square yard is enclosed by high walls with a square tower at each corner and is surrounded by barns, milking parlours and stables. Sandwell Metropolitan Borough operates the site as a model farm with old breeds in residence, exhibitions and refreshment facilities. Park Farm Wood, which lies between the motorway and the farm, is rich in natural history. Well over 100 species of fungi have been recorded there including a number of *Cortinarius* species amongst which is *Cortinarius urbicus*, an unusual toadstool associated with grey poplar. A couple of interesting trees growing in the wood are a cut-leaved beech and a Lucombe oak. The latter is a variety of the Spanish oak, which is itself a hybrid between the Turkey and the cork oak. The cut-leaved beech is a less common variety than the ubiquitous copper beech. Its leaves are deeply cut, almost fern-like, but this specimen shows the widespread phenomenon affecting this hybrid in that one branch has reverted to type and has the usual beech leaves. This is normally accounted for by damage to the branch concerned.

On the route through the kissing gate evidence of the parkland which was laid out around here will be seen. A plant beloved of landscape gardeners – rhododendron ('tree rose') – forms dense thickets in many places. Apart from providing roosting sites for small birds on cold winter nights it has virtually no wildlife value at all. One of the earls of Dartmouth did service abroad including a spell in North America and, being interested in trees, took the opportunity to introduce a number of exotic and unusual species to the estate. Two have already been mentioned and to these can be added swamp cypress, holm oak and false acacia. The latter two are seen growing together just past the wooden bridge to the right of the path. The cypress and the false acacia (locust tree) are from America whilst the holm (evergreen) oak is from Southern Europe. The evergreen oak is easily spotted during winter months by its dark-green foliage. The bark is cracked into small squares in marked contrast to the deeply-fissured bark of the neighbouring false acacia.

Passing these and other trees, including yews, an incredibly contorted horse chestnut will be seen on the right. It stands guardian over a small pool within which grows the swamp cypress. This is a deciduous conifer whose needles turn a beautiful russet colour in autumn. It is the last tree in the valley to come into leaf each year, often showing no more than token greenery well into June. Along one side of this pool grows greater spearwort, our largest yellow buttercup and which is rare in the Midlands. This is one of only half a dozen places in Staffordshire where it is known to grow wild.

The pool has a population of fine carp. In mid-summer they can often be seen spawning in the shallow water, their plump dark bodies shimmering and seething as they splash around. They need warm water to spawn successfully and the shallowness of this

Greater spearwort

pool helps to provide this at the critical time. For the rest of the year they are quiet, almost invisible, inhabitants of the pool – at least as far as people are concerned. This is partly because they feed at night – and no doubt the insect larvae and crustaceans on which they feed look upon them as being all too prominent. In turn the young carp provide dinner for the great-crested grebe chicks from the adjacent pool. The adult grebes may be seen flying from one pool to the other delivering fresh fish by the minute to their voracious offspring.

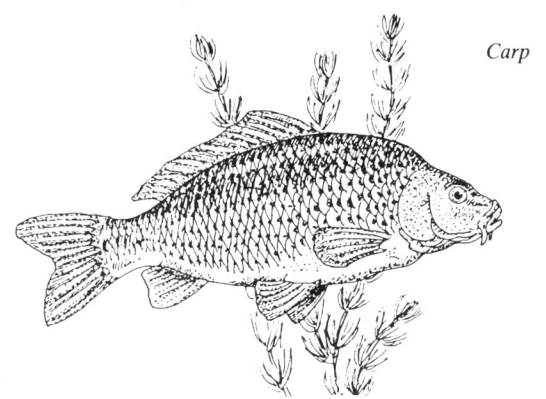

Carp

> *Despite its carnivorous habits the carp has no teeth in its mouth. They are behind its gills in the pharynx, a characteristic common to all members of this family.*

Grebes share the two larger pools with a variety of waterfowl, including mallard, tufted duck, pochard, coot and, occasionally, ruddy duck. The latter, which is an introduction from America, has now become naturalised and is mainly encountered in the Midlands. It has a white face and blue bill, and is a member of the group of ducks called 'stiff-tails' – indeed it is quite easily recognised by its habit of swimming with tail cocked-up. With those other Americans, the swamp cypress and the grey squirrel, for company it probably feels quite at home here.

Ruddy ducks

The ditch which the path crosses is another reminder of the 18th-century parkland. It is the remains of a ha-ha – a subtle means of controlling deer movements without introducing unsightly landscape features such as fences. The ha-ha was a cutting around the formal gardens close to the hall, higher and steeper on the side facing outwards from the garden. Therefore, when looking out from the hall, the deer could be seen peacefully grazing in the parkland, but could not get into the garden and damage the ornamental flowers.

Walking towards Swan Pool – with the flashing lights of Sutton Coldfield television mast in the distance – the northern part of the valley is seen laid out. To the left the fields of Hill House Farm tumble down the hill and to the right horses graze in the meadows. Another old sweet chestnut stands in the field, not far from the gaunt fingers of an oak which was struck by lightning in 1985.

Cross the wide track (if having arrived from Park Farm, turn left here) and cross the field towards the poplars, keeping the water on the left. Go over a wooden bridge and walk half right towards the last poplar on the right. Cross the road and, following the 'Beacon Way' signs to the left, walk to the river.

The grazed horse pastures are the haunt of wheatears as they pass through the valley on migration, whilst the rough grassland around Swan Pool is permanently filled with skylarks and meadow pipits. The pipits rise up with a few feeble 'tseep-tseeps', providing no competition to the mellifluous skylarks. In summer the field is also populated with meadow brown butterflies. At any time of the year the gaudy sails of dinghies and sailboards scurry to and fro on the pool. A few birds congregate morosely around the small island, a reminder of the much larger numbers found here when the pool was 'derelict'. The landscape was not so pleasant then but there were reedmace swamp, willow carr and alder trees. When it was all cleared away and the pool enlarged it was hailed as a great improvement. The reed buntings did not do much cheering though!

When the road is crossed, and depending on the time of the year, look out for either brilliant-red berries or white flowers in the hedge bordering the golf course. Close inspection will reveal not only the guelder rose which might be anticipated, but also some cotoneaster. The latter can now be added to the already long list of non-native species introduced to the valley during the past 300 years.

The large lake which now appears was constructed in the early 1980s to help control flooding along the River Tame. It is the second largest body of open water in the area, only Chasewater being bigger, and is already established as being of vital importance to wintering waterfowl. Its size means that open water remains available when many smaller pools are frozen over. In January and February the flock of birds will probably include mute swan, Canada goose, teal, wigeon, tufted duck, mallard, pochard, goldeneye, coot, and great-crested grebe. A whooper swan turned up for the first time in the 1986/7 winter, gracing the valley with its presence before returning to the far north of Europe to breed. Whoopers are easily distinguished from our resident mute swans by their black-tipped yellow bills. If you think swans are pure white then look at them when there is snow on the ground – they appear decidedly off-white. Ice on the pool, snow on the banks, sparkling sunshine on the multi-coloured plumage of birds – these combine to create a scene worth travelling miles to enjoy. If the cold gets too much, a warm welcome awaits on the far side of the lake at the first ever urban reserve of the Royal Society for the Protection of Birds.

Turn right to follow the river bank as it curves round the lake. Turn right again over the wooden bridge and follow the path uphill with the golf course on the right. Turn right at the metalled road and then left to go around to the back of the building. Take the path to the trees on top of the hill.

Spare a thought for the poor old River Tame, channelled here between high artificial banks and having to run where it never did before. For nearly a hundred centuries it meandered gently along, its crystal waters fringed with reeds, alders, osiers and willows. Then came farmers who cultivated its flood-plain, followed by mill owners who usurped its power and diverted the water into head-and-tail races, then industrialists who polluted it, and, finally, water engineers who dictated where it should run. The lot of an urban river is not a happy one!

As well as waterfowl this part of the valley is noted for the waders which pop in for a few days on their annual migration. Redshank, greenshank, dunlin, ruff, snipe, common sandpiper, ringed plover and oystercatcher have all been recorded. Recently, a couple of redshank liked their bed-and-breakfast stop-over so much that they set up home and tried to breed, unfortunately without success. Places such as this are very important to these long-distance travellers who are greatly helped by the chance to rest, feed, and to find refuge from bad weather during their journeys.

Pausing on the bridge on a still day, the pool on the right will perfectly reflect the sky and trees. One's own reflections will be accompanied by the gentle trickle of water over the twisted stems of some half-fallen willows. At dusk in summer bats hunt all around here – tiny pipistrelles and their larger cousins, noctules, are present in the valley. The noctules are known to roost in tree-holes in the vicinity of Cypress Pool. As the last swallows and martins peel gracefully away to roost in the fading light the bats appear. Where the birds glide and swoop with consummate ease, the bats seem to flitter and flutter uncertainly. Don't be fooled, however, they are no less masters of the air. Although they both eat flying insects, competition between the birds and the bats is avoided because they hunt at different times. Birds solve the problem of the winter scarcity of flying insects by migrating; the bats do so by hibernating. The different lifestyles thus adopted illustrate very well the natural mechanisms which have evolved to reduce competition between species exploiting the same food source. Bats are very strange creatures indeed, and it is odd to remember that they are built more in the way of whales than birds. In turn whales are more like bats than fish. In each case it is their habits which closely approach those of the other group, not their physical characteristics.

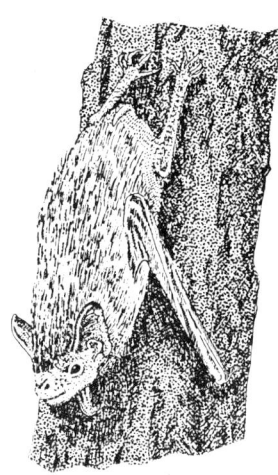

Noctule bat

In the middle of the golf course on the right Manwoods Farm once stood. Although unremarkable in itself, it is noteworthy as the place at which a man whose preaching was to help to shape a nation first practised the art. He was the young Francis Asbury who became the first bishop of the Methodist church in America. The only permanent home he ever knew was a cottage in nearby Newton Road which is now a museum devoted to his memory and is visited each year by many Americans. A statue of Asbury was unveiled in Washington in 1924 by President Coolidge.

Bishop Asbury never had a home in America for 45 years. During that time he travelled over 250,000 miles on horseback. He lived out of a saddle bag, the very opposite of so many members of today's materialistic society.

On the way up the hill look out on the left for a curious feature which is actually a bracken hedge. A strip of the original heathland has survived between the golf courses in the form of a small bank. The dominant plant on this is bracken, although rushes grow in the dampness at its base.

Turn left at the path by the trees and right, after a few yards, up the final incline along a metalled path. Follow the path round to the right through the derelict gun emplacements.

By the time the beech and oak trees on top of the hill are reached a climb of about 150 feet from the river will have been achieved. This area is aptly named Hill Top, being the highest part of the valley, and is at the edge of the Birmingham Plateau. The old bunkers are reminders of the anti-aircraft guns positioned here during the the Second World War. No peaceful walks then as the fire raining from the sky was met by that from the guns. Nowadays, the defence of places like this takes a different form but in its own way is no less important. Birmingham's rebuilt city centre rises to the south with the Telecommunications tower, the digital clock of the Post and Mail building, and the red neon of the Rotunda, all being prominent. Slightly to the west, but closer, is the church of Handsworth Cemetery – built in imitation of Lichfield Cathedral. The long grey roofs of the terraced houses in Handsworth lead to the white soffit boards of newer houses immediately in front. These are, in fact, the first houses on this part of the northern fringe of Birmingham – the spot where the city was stopped by the countryside.

The oaks around Hill Top are home to one of our prettiest but most elusive butterflies, the purple hairstreak. It is not common in the Midlands, and is always difficult to see because of its habit of flying weakly around the treetops; it is also single brooded and only on the wing in July and August. The caterpillars feed on oak leaves and when fully fed have a long trek down the tree trunk to pupate either under moss, leaf litter or, more rarely, in a crack in the bark. When their food is not available, bats hibernate and swallows migrate – purple hairstreaks spend the winter as eggs nestling in the buds of oaks. This intimate association with their food-plant obviously makes them very vulnerable to woodland management when that involves the felling of oaks and this no doubt explains their association with ancient and relatively undisturbed oak woods. The purple hairstreak's survival here is somewhat unexpected but all the more welcome for that.

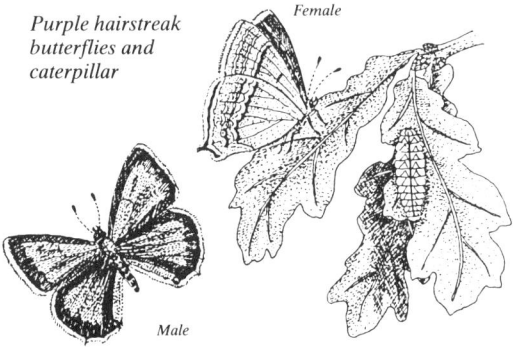

Purple hairstreak butterflies and caterpillar

Female

Male

Turn left at the tarmac path and follow it around the football pitches and through the small wood to where the walk started at the car park.

Starlings, wood-pigeons and magpies all abound here. The white flash of a jay's rump may be seen, or the undulating flight of a green woodpecker. Through the wood, beech, elder, hawthorn and holly line the path. Underfoot during November the path will be covered in yellowish discs. These are probably dismissed by most as seeds, but close inspection would reveal that they are the red spangles which covered the undersides of oak leaves in September. They are galls and inside each one is the larva of a tiny wasp. Wasps lay their eggs in leaf tissue and the hatching of the grub causes the tree to produce 'extra' tissue. This envelops the grub and serves to protect it and to supply its food. Unlike the snail, which moves about with its house on its back, the wasp larvae stay put but eat the house instead. It is not entirely protected as some other wasps sometimes pierce the gall wall to lay their own eggs inside. Their offspring then either eat the gall tissue in place of the rightful owner, or the rightful owner itself, which seems a bit unsporting. Even if the gall wasp escapes these fates it is still at risk from birds, particularly pheasants, who have developed a taste for these tiny natural 'meat pies'. The spangle galls are only one type of several dozen such growths which oaks support.

> Many oak galls are rich in tannin, an important constituent of inks and dyes. This frequently made them a marketable commodity. The first charter granted by Charles I to the East India Company permitted them to import galls.

SALTWELLS WOOD

Doulton's Claypit – designated a Site of Special Scientific Interest

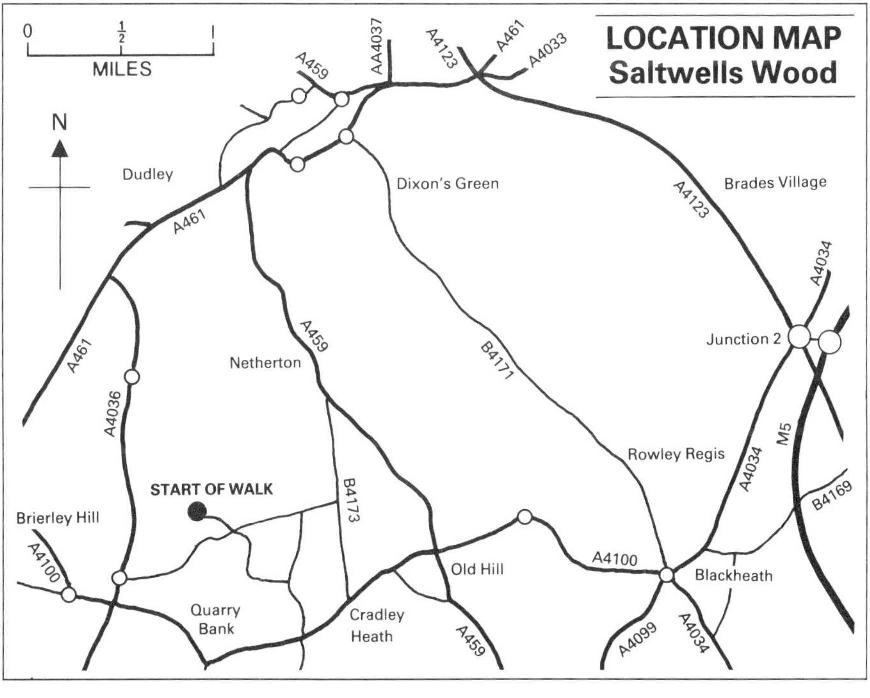

**LOCATION MAP
Saltwells Wood**

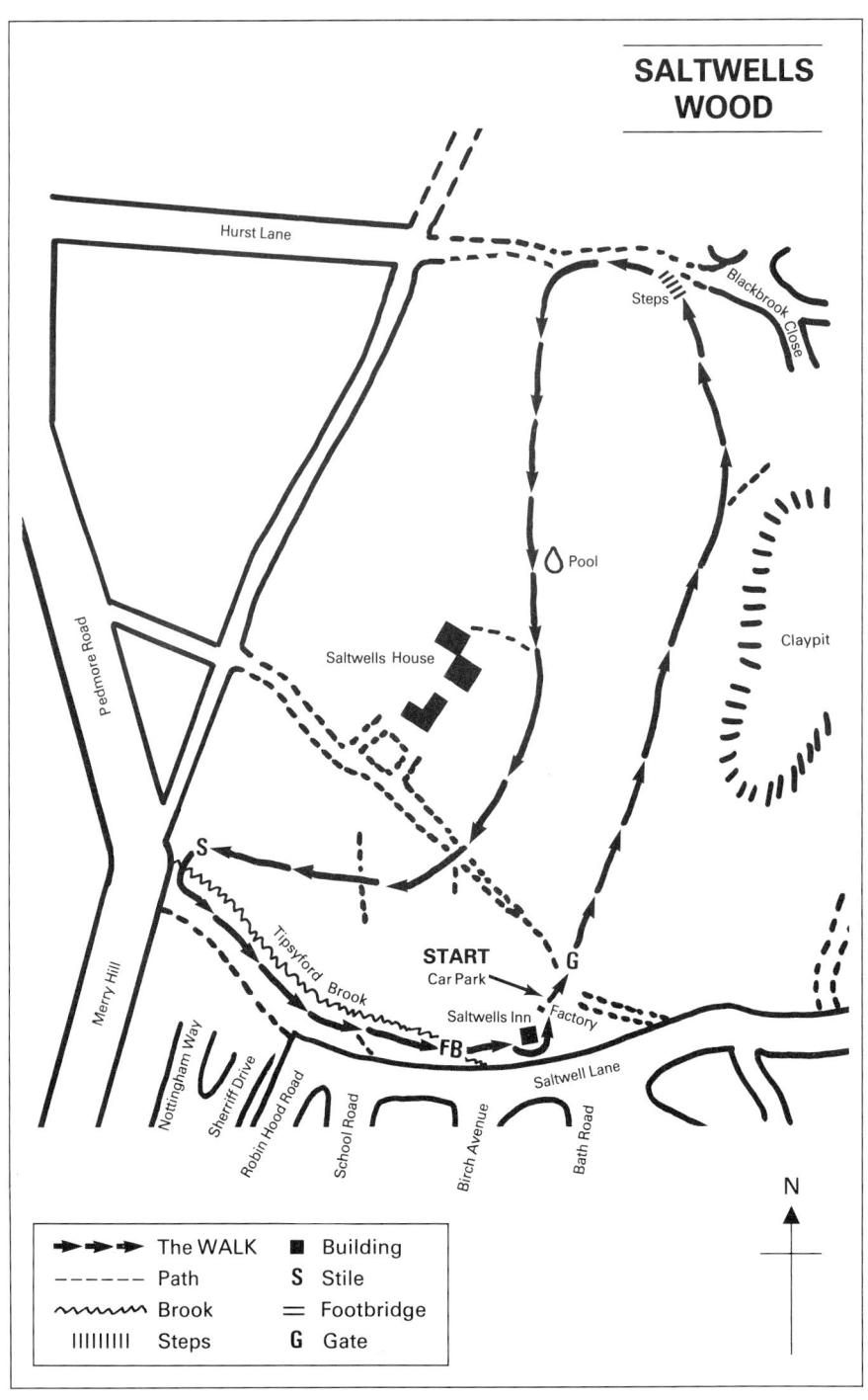

SALTWELLS WOOD

O.S. SO98 (1:25000) – 932868   Approx. 1½ miles

An undulating walk on good paths, but including the descent of a flight of about 65 well-made steps. Can be wet in parts.

This is a wonderfully varied woodland in the heart of the Black Country. Its history is as rich as wildlife, and the geology of the adjacent disused claypit is of such value that it has been notified as a Site of Special Scientific Interest (SSSI). The wood and the claypit together were declared the first Local Nature Reserve in the county of West Midlands in September 1981. There is a great contrast between the open aspect around the lip of the claypit and the dark recesses of the wood. Although many of the trees now present were planted about 200 years ago, woodland has probably been on the site for many centuries. Early coal mines were sunk long before the Industrial Revolution in order to preserve the timber for purposes other than fuelling furnaces.

Follow the signs off Saltwells Road to Saltwells Inn and park either in the reserve car park (open until 4.30 pm) or on the space between the car park and the inn. Opposite the small factory, go through a five-bar gate entrance. Walk straight ahead past the claypit on the right.

Near this path on a summer's evening, the song thrushes, silhouetted on post, tree and chimney, 'calling the tune' to each other in an avian song contest, may find themselves in competition with the changes being rung by the bellringers of the local church. Add to this the efforts of willow warblers and wrens, an occasional snort or whinny from the horses in the meadow, and you will be able to close your eyes and allow yourself to be transported in an aural time machine to whichever of the last few centuries takes your fancy. This same combination of sounds could have been heard when Saltwells Wood was but a small corner of Pensnett Chase and the industry which changed the name of the area to the Black Country was still to come. The tides of history may have flowed over and around this last remaining fragment of a once-great forest stretching from Cannock in the north to the Wyre Forest in the south, but rock-like it is here still.

To the right of the path is a stand of blackthorn, heavy in early June with young green sloes holding the promise of the juicy purple ripeness to follow. They are a reminder that even at the height of the growing sea-

Bluebell fruits

son with mid-summer still approaching, early flowering plants have already set their fruits. The bluebells too are almost over now and in place of the brilliant-blue carpets beneath the trees there is now a miniature forest of green bobbles, inside which the black seeds are developing. The blackthorn leaves are covered with hundreds of white pustules. These galls are caused by tiny relatives of the spider, called gall mites, which live inside the pustules, so gaining a degree of protection from predators. On the left of this path is a meadow, golden with buttercups in summer, which in bygone days was the venue for the local Sunday schools' annual outing. No doubt those children, and their parents and grandparents before them, used the same field for 'mayings' (making daisy chains and cowslip balls), and in autumn they would have roamed the hedgerows on nut-gathering expeditions.

Almost without warning the land to the right of the path falls away and a stunning view of Doulton's Claypit is revealed. As its name suggests this mighty excavation, now about 50 feet shallower than it used to be after partial infilling, was used to supply clay to Doultons (of fine china fame). The mineral taken from here was not destined for the dining rooms of high society, however, but for the bathrooms – it was used in the making of sanitary earthenware and clay pipes. Since clayworking ceased in the 1940s the slopes of the pit have become clothed in shrubs and trees, consisting mainly of birch, oak and hawthorn. The bottom of the pit has developed a wonderful collection of flowers such as marsh orchids and yellow flag. Even from a vantage point high above, the bright-yellow flowers of the latter can easily be picked out.

> *The flowers of yellow flag are said to be the original Fleur-de-Lis emblem of France. A fanciful resemblance of the flowers to frogs led to that English nickname for the French.*

The most spectacular feature of the claypit, and the reason for its designation as an SSSI, are the sections of exposed rock showing the different layers which underly the area. Each level shows where succeeding tropical swamps played host to plants and creatures even more varied and fantastic than those enjoying our more temperate climate today. The nearest face to the footpath looks exactly like that – a 'face', with dark eyebrows and a flat nose, very similar to those impassive statues bequeathed to the world by the lost peoples of Easter Island.

> *The area around Dudley is so rich in fossils that a trilobite is incorporated into the town's coat-of-arms, surely the only such geological heraldry in the country. It is called by the locals 'The Dudley Bug'.*

Agile walkers can easily climb down into the claypit and out again to rejoin the path.

Turn left up a ramp by a sycamore tree on to a flat open area, go straight across and descend a long flight of steps, turning left at the bottom.

In late May and early June young birds are everywhere, their cheeps and chirps reminding harassed parents that even though their offspring can get out of the nest they still expect to be fed. The adults flit through the grass and trees, delivering morsel after morsel to the insatiable youngsters. Great tits, blue tits, blackbirds, wood-pigeons, jays and woodpeckers may all be seen around here.

The jays are probably responsible for many of the young oaks growing on the claypit slopes, thanks to their habit of collecting acorns in autumn and burying them. No doubt these hidden stores are intended to supplement a meagre diet in the depths of winter and, though some of them must be found again, many remain safe from further attention to grow up in their new resting place.

The flat area – locally called the 'table-top' – is the top of one of the spoil heaps which was thrown up when the pit was excavated and used as a football pitch by the workers. Today it is dotted with ox-eye daisies (moon pennies), and takes on a soft-red hue because of the low-growing flowers of sheep's sorrel. The bright-yellow flowers of mouse-ear hawkweed and the white umbels of elder add more colour to the scene. At the top of the steps a distant view of Netherton Top Church perched upon the next hill will be glimpsed. Closer to hand the insistent 'chiffchaff, chiffchaff' of that small warbler coming from below brings the realisation that just here the route is in the treetops. A pause literally provides a bird's-eye view through the branches of the woodland canopy. Such a sight demonstrates how surprising it is that birds can navigate through the tangled maze of foliage without constantly colliding with branches and twigs. At the foot of the steps, on the left, there is a dark and mysterious woodscape where ivy scrambles over the ground beneath a low, dense canopy of hawthorn, whilst on the right there is another meadow gleaming brightly with a million buttercups.

Take the left fork, passing the pool on the left. At the T-junction turn left.

Soft pink dog roses mark the way here and moths, flowerbugs, bees and hoverflies make their own erratic journeys through the wood. Dragonflies and damselflies also frequent this area, the pool having been re-excavated recently so that it can continue to provide a home for their nymphs. Great diving beetles, frogs and toads breed here in Snake Pool, as it is called – a name not at all fanciful because there is a thriving colony of grass snakes in this part of Saltwells Wood. These harmless reptiles are one of only three species of snake found wild in Britain. No confusion between the species is likely in the Midlands because as regards the other two, the smooth snake is restricted to southern counties and the poisonous adder (viper) has an unmistakable dark zig-zag stripe down its back. The flowers may be different but these lines by Shakespeare sit well on the scene here.

I know a bank whereon the wild thyme blows,
Where ox-lips and the nodding violet grows;
Quite over-canopied with lush woodbine,
With sweet musk roses, and with eglantine:

There sleeps Titania some time of the night,
Lull'd in these flowers with dances and delight;
And there the snake throws her enamell'd skin,
Weed wide enough to wrap a fairy in.

From *A Midsummer Night's Dream*, by William Shakespeare

Grass snakes are also called ringed snakes because of the prominent 'collar' round the neck but like most amphibians and reptiles there is a great variation in colouring between individuals, in this case mostly differences of olive greens, browns and greys. They have a preference for watery places and the population here probably feeds mainly on frogs, although toads, newts, tadpoles, young birds and small mammals will also be taken. They will catch and eat food both in and out of the water. The general lack of snakes in this country is due to the

> The constant flicking in and out of a snake's tongue is an additional way of smelling. When inside the forked tongue fits into a depression in the roof of the mouth called Jacobson's organ, a sort of second nose.

Grass snake

fact that they are cold-blooded and need the warmth of the sun to bring them up to 'working temperature'. This is no doubt a factor contributing to the well-known habit of the females to seek out warm spots like compost heaps, piles of sawdust, hayricks or piles of leaves in which to lay eggs – only one other species in Europe, the Aesculapian snake, deliberately searches for such artificial egg-laying sites. Grass snakes give up the unequal struggle with our climate altogether in winter and hibernate from late October to early March.

Snakes have one thing in common with fish (apart from being scaly) – they grow in length during the course of tale-telling! The longest recorded grass snakes in Europe are about six-and-a-half feet, and just under six feet in Britain, with the average being three to four feet. People will always swear that the ones they have seen are at least six feet!

An ideal place for the local snakes to lurk is the area of rushes by the side of the pool. These plants are particularly associated with damp places with poor soil. They are smooth with narrow cylindrical leaves growing in tufts, and tight heads or clusters of brownish or greenish flowers. These flower-heads sometimes seem to grow from the sides of the stems but this is not so – the apparent continuation of the stem above is a bract, a leaf-like structure that usually appears beneath the flowers on other species.

> Botanists are unable to distinguish the petals and sepals of the flowers of some plants, including rush. They call the offending parts 'tepals' instead.

Just after passing under an overhanging beech bough look out for an oak stump, about three feet high, sprouting at the top. Walk on a few yards and it becomes apparent that something very strange has happened here; there are hundreds of small stumps like this by the path, very thin and sprouting even thinner branches from their tops. This place could be called 'Firewood Coppice' because the local population used this part of the wood for many years, until the early 1980s, as a source of free firewood. The cutting was mostly done by young lads, hence the resulting short thin stumps.

At the five ways take the path second right and, further on, carry straight ahead at the crossroads. Go over the stile and turn left across the concrete lintel spanning the stream.

Green hairstreak butterflies

The clearing where the five paths meet is a good place for watching butterflies in summer. About two dozen types have been found in the wood including speckled wood, and both green and purple hairstreak. The latter keeps itself in regal isolation near to the top of oak trees for most of the time and so is not often encountered. The speckled wood on the other hand is very easy to spot as it basks on a sunny bramble leaf showing off its cream-spotted brown wings. Basking it may appear to be but it is uncanny how as soon as another speckled wood passes close by, the owner of the territory 'scrambles' and flies to meet the intruder. There follows a graceful aerial *pas de deux* as the two pirouette skywards in what presumably must be a butterfly fight. The incomer invariably retreats allowing the occupier to regain the bramble leaf, adjust its gumshield and make ready for the next round. This poet summed up the average butterfly's aerial ability in these lines:

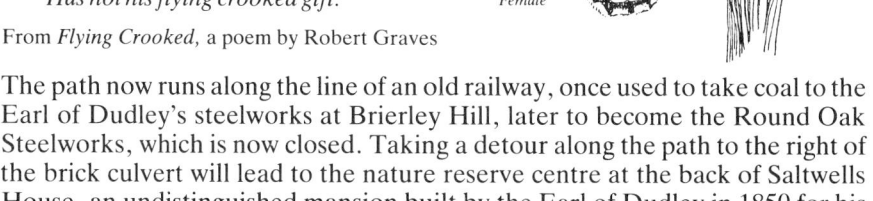

Speckled wood butterflies
Male
Female

> The butterfly, a cabbage-white,
> (His honest idiocy of flight)
> Will never now, it is too late,
> Master the art of flying straight,
> Yet has – who knows so well as I? –
>
> A just sense of how not to fly:
> He lurches here and there by guess
> And God and hope and hopelessness
> Even the aerobatic swift
> Has not his flying crooked gift.

From *Flying Crooked,* a poem by Robert Graves

The path now runs along the line of an old railway, once used to take coal to the Earl of Dudley's steelworks at Brierley Hill, later to become the Round Oak Steelworks, which is now closed. Taking a detour along the path to the right of the brick culvert will lead to the nature reserve centre at the back of Saltwells House, an undistinguished mansion built by the Earl of Dudley in 1850 for his

Greater stitchwort

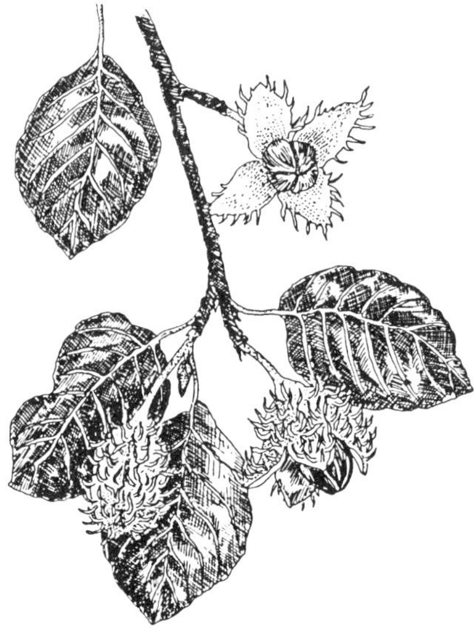

Beech mast

wife. She apparently never took to the house and it was occupied by the keeper of the wood. The centre itself, operated by Dudley Council, is well worth visiting for its displays and information about the wood.

The yellow flowers and red spiky fruits of wood avens intertwine with greater stitchwort, cleavers, and the evil-smelling hedge woundwort along here, all overlooked by the flat-topped flower-heads of hogweed. A pyramid of ivy covers an old tree-stump making it look like an 'ivy tree', whilst overhead newly-formed beech mast is developing. Woodpeckers, nuthatches and tree creepers are birds typical of this area. The nuthatches make use of old woodpecker holes to nest in, the two streams which run nearby providing the mud they use to make the entrance hole smaller.

Amongst the moths of Saltwells Wood is a beautiful tiny triangular moth, bronze in colour with a broad yellow stripe across its wings. The male is unmistakable because of its enorm-

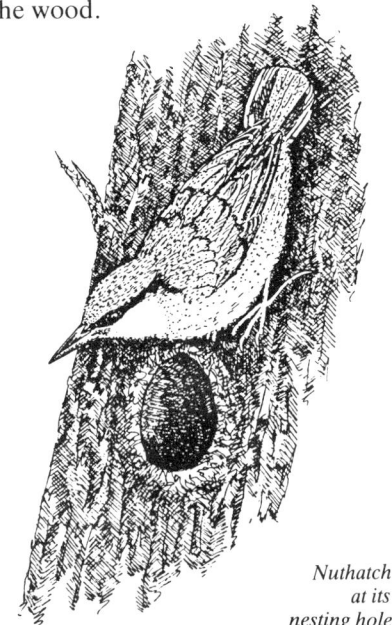

Nuthatch at its nesting hole

ously long feelers, many times longer than its body, which make it the longest moth in Britain. This attractive creature has no common name and has to bear the burden of being called *Nemephora degeerella*, although sometimes the group to which it belongs is called 'bright moths'.

Once over the stile the open, disturbed ground provides an ideal place for opportunistic flowers like spear thistle, colt's-foot with its large flat leaves, and hairy tare which scrambles up and over its neighbours. The stream is the Tipsyford Brook, a name said to be associated with the large number of public houses hereabout – too much of the local brew resulting in an unscheduled dip in the stream on the way home.

Turn left just where the steps come down from the road on the right. Walk straight on keeping the stream on the left. Go through two five-bar gateways and over a footbridge.

The stream is screened at first by an old hedge, close inspection of which reveals that it is mainly composed of privet. It is the remains of a garden hedge which belonged to a cottage which stood by the Tipsyford Brook. On the other side of the path deep shadows hide the interior of the woodland, bringing an air of mystery and darkness. In some places around here grows the plant with perhaps the most magical name of any in Britain, enchanter's nightshade. Curiously it is not a nightshade at all but a willowherb, sending up spikes of tiny white flowers. It is often in fruit at the base of the stem whilst still in bud at the top. This characteristic can be seen displayed by its more prominent cousin, rosebay willowherb. Anywhere along here water voles may be seen and occasionally, it is said, mink will be encountered. These American relatives of weasels and stoats are now firmly established in many parts of the country, having escaped from fur farms earlier this century. They always live close to water as fish forms a major part of their diet.

Enchanter's nightshade

This part of the wood is close to the site of the enterprise which gave it the name of Saltwells. (It has been variously called part of Pensnett Chase, Ladywood and Casson's Wood, the latter being the name of one of the keepers who lived at Saltwells House.) Long before the Industrial Revolution the whole area was used for supplies of timber, clay and coal. One unsuccessful coal mining venture may have led to the discovery of brine as the pit flooded and became unworkable. In *The Natural History of Staffordshire* by Robert Plot, published in 1636, the following appears:

In Pensnet Chase *south from* Dudley *about a mile and a half there is another* weak brine *belonging to the right* Honorable Edward *Lord* Ward *of which his* Lordship *once attempted to make* salt; *but the* brine *proving too* weak, *he thought fit to desist, though possibly it might have been advanced to profit by the* Art *of* Tunnelling *much used in* Cheshire *to keep out the* freshes.

Extract quoted in *The Saltwells Near Dudley,* by E. Blocksidge

Making salt by evaporation may not have been profitable but operating baths in later centuries certainly was. Saltwells became a spa, the most important in this part of the Midlands, and people travelled from miles away to 'take the waters'. As recently as 1900 a local analyst and chemist wrote to Mr Flavell, then licensee of the Saltwells Inn, 'From these figures you will see that the water is of a very remarkable character. It is very similar in composition to the well-known Woodhall Spa [Lincolnshire] water which bears a high reputation for medicinal properties'. Mr Flavell could apparently supply cold baths and water for medicinal purposes at very short notice, but a hot bath had to be booked by letter. The first Sunday in May was traditionally the day of Saltwells Wake when large numbers of people used to visit to 'take the waters' and stroll through the wood, as we do today, 'taking the air'.

At the Saltwells Inn turn left between the inn and the houses to return to the car park.

This short path between the buildings is not without olfactory merit at certain times of the year and certain times of the day. On the left may be the warm smells of cooking for the inn's patrons, whilst on the right can be the soft perfume of honeysuckle covering the garden wall. The licensee believes the visitor can obtain further pleasure from this walk by sampling his brews, but brine is no longer on the bill of fare.

Mink

SUTTON PARK

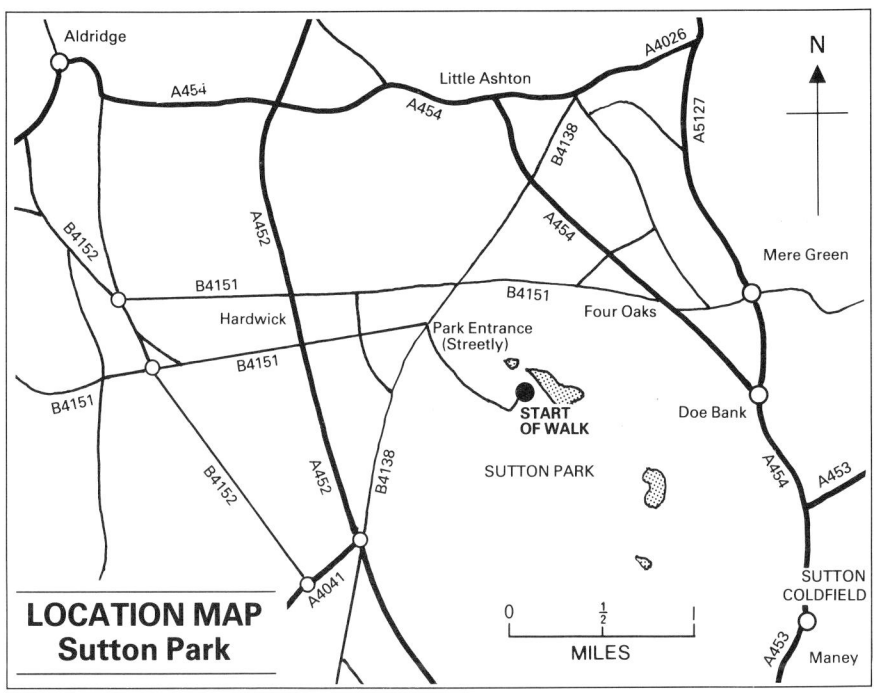

**LOCATION MAP
Sutton Park**

O.S. SP09 (1:25000) – 095980　　　　　　　　　　Approx. 2¾ miles

An undulating walk through heath and woodland in the richest area for natural history in the county of West Midlands. Very wet in places.

Sutton Park is a nationally important wildlife site being 2,500 acres of wood, heath, and wetland. It has never been enclosed in the usual sense of the word but it is bounded by a perimeter fence, and is one of the largest fenced parks in Europe. It is home to many plants and animals, some of them rare in the locality. Once a royal hunting ground the park now hosts over one million visitors a year; despite this it is possible to find the seclusion needed to appreciate fully its unique landscapes. This walk takes in one of the quiet corners, passing only briefly by one of the 'honeypots'. It goes through a cross-section of the most important habitats and gives the opportunity to enjoy both the abundant wildlife and the incomparable scenery.

Enter the park through Streetly Gate in Thornhill Road. Turn left along the very wide unmetalled track leading to the edge of some woodland. Park near the fence and go through the five-bar gate and over the railway bridge. Follow the path round to the left to turn right over the little three-arched bridge.　　　31

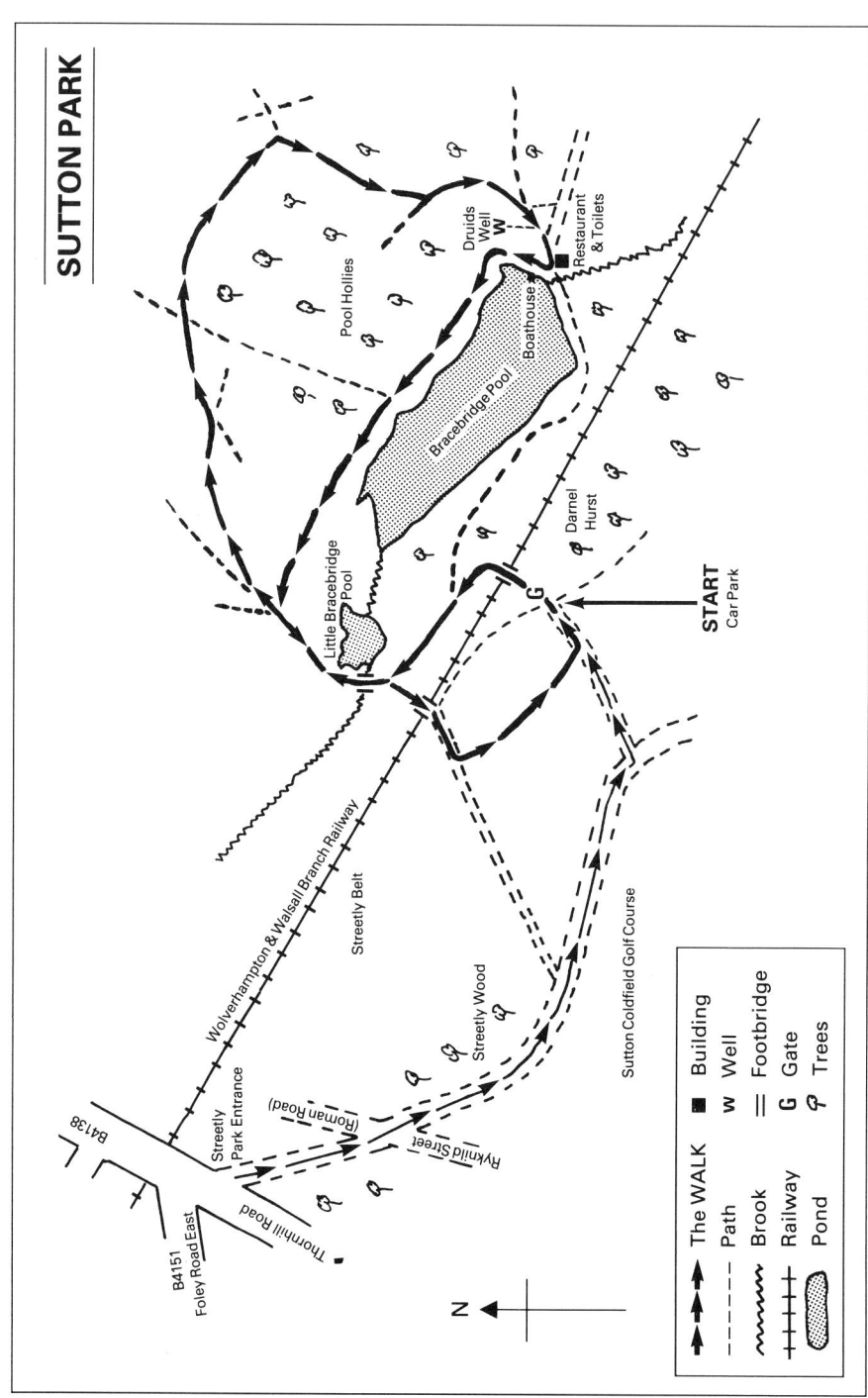

Holly, beech, rowan, oak and pine line the way with the wind whispering through their branches. A carpet of soft brown leaves lies either side of the pebbly path with bright green bracken fronds nodding above. The heady fragrance of pine wafts through the air, birds sing overhead, and ripe rowan berries dangle in gaudy opulence – each sense in turn accosted by the living woodland, as they must have been for over a thousand years ever since Sutton Park has been both a home for wildlife and a playground for people.

Once part of a great forest joining Cannock Chase, the Wyre Forest and the Forest of Arden, where bear, wolf and boar roamed, it remains an isolated remnant of ancient landscapes, altered and abused but not entirely eradicated. This 'royal forest' became a 'chase' in 802 when the King of Mercia was demoted to the status of earl following the uniting of the Saxon kingdoms; only a king could hunt in a royal forest, an earl had to make do with a chase. When a later earl lost his lands to William the Conqueror the area was a royal forest once more until a deal between Henry I and the Earl of Warwick in 1126 made it a chase again. After Warwick the Kingmaker fell at the Battle of Barnet near the end of the Wars of the Roses Henry VII confiscated his lands and the site's status changed once again. This royal ping-pong was finally ended in 1528 when one of Sutton's sons – John Harman, Bishop of Exeter and an associate of Henry VIII – obtained a royal charter for the town, purchased the land and then gave it to the townspeople in perpetuity. Although its boundaries have altered several times since, the land has remained open, grazed but not generally cultivated or agriculturally improved. It has been used for hunting, horse racing, boating, fairs, pageants and jamborees. The military, from the archers of Crecy and Agincourt to the tank troops of the Second World War, have used it for camping and training. Some of the wildlife has disappeared (badgers, woodcock, primroses and violets quite recently) but much has survived including about 20 wildflower species which grow here and nowhere else in Warwickshire.

Having crossed the railway where it runs in a deep cutting be prepared for the shock of seeing a locomotive suddenly appear roaring through the trees on the left – the change in level being greater than is apparent. With such a rude interruption out of the way, look out for the first glimpse of Little Bracebridge Pool's limpid and tranquil waters through the wood to the right. The scene could have been tailor-made for this poem by A. A. Milne called *The Mirror*.

Between the woods the afternoon
Is fallen in a golden swoon.
The sun looks down from quiet skies
To where a quiet water lies,
And silent trees stoop down to trees.

And there I saw a white swan make
Another white swan in the lake;
And, breast to breast, both motionless,
They waited for the wind's caress . . .
And all the water was at ease.

From *When We Were Very Young*, by A. A. Milne

As the path approaches the end of the pool the ground ahead is seen to be studded with the upturned golden star-like flowers of lesser spearwort, one of our most attractive buttercups. Above them bob the blue pom-poms of devil's-bit scabious, alas no longer providing fodder for the caterpillars of marsh fritillary butterflies which now do not breed in the park.

33

Devil's-bit scabious

> Devil's-bit scabious is a popular herb that owes its name to the shape of its root which appears to have a piece broken off. It was said that the devil, begrudging its usefulness to man, had taken a bite out of it.

Sulphur tuft

Turn right over the three-arched bridge past the end of the pool. Further on where the path splits into three take the middle way and almost immediately take the right-hand fork by the oak tree. Continue on past the divided birch with callus and turn left at the crossways and up a slight rise.

The crude concrete and brick structures are completely out of place in this beautiful corner. Little Bracebridge Pool is fringed with yellow flag, its broad green leaves, tipped brown in late summer, contrasting with the emerald green patches of the bogbean foliage. The dark recesses on the far side of the water often accommodate ghostly grey herons, and in summer the pool is filled with the yellow flowers of fringed water-lily.

It is possible to enjoy the landscape over the pool without any artefacts intruding at all: no fences, wires, buildings, pylons or chimneys offend the eye. The view, though shaped by man's activities, is completely natural; it is possible to feel more alone in this apparently remote wilderness than it is on the high tops of the Lake District or North Wales. A similar illusion can be recreated a little further on by looking to the left, over the rough grass and heather.

This part of the walk passes by young oak, birch and holly woodland and offers an abundance of fungi. Large numbers of yellow toadstools with darker centres to their caps clustered on an old stump may catch the eye. They are sulphur tuft, and can be seen at any time of the year and are claimed by some to be the most common species in the country. Fly agaric – the archetypal red and white toadstool often found in association with birch – is here as are the russula and boletus species. All but the latter have fleshy folds called gills

Fly agaric contains a powerful hallucinatory substance and is the 'magic' mushroom of folklore. It is said to be the divine mushroom of immortality used in early religions.

running in parallel along the undersides of their caps; it is here that the reproductive spores are generated. Boletus species make their spores in tubes which hang vertically beneath the cap and have pores at the bottom to allow them to escape. This arrangement gives them a sponge-like appearance. One of the group, *Boletus edulis* – variously known as the 'cep', the 'penny-bun boletus', and (particularly in France and Italy) as the 'king of mushrooms' – is said to be very good eating indeed. Also growing in the vicinity is the chantarelle, another culinary delight often used commercially for packet soups. It has a hollow cap with the gills running down the upper part of the stem, or stipe as it is more properly called.

People are much more hesitant about eating wild fungi in this country than the inhabitants of the rest of Europe and this is probably wise. There are many kinds which are dangerous, even fatal, to eat and they can be difficult to separate from edible look-alikes.

All fungi exist either as parasites on living organisms or as saprophytes on dead material where they act as agents of decay. Possessing no chlorophyll they are unable to utilise the energy of the sun to build tissue. Fungi obtain their nutrients 'second-hand', being neither 'producers' like green plants nor 'consumers' like plant-eaters. They are classed as 'reducers' and play a key role in the recycling of life-building substances. The spore-producing fruiting body which we call a mushroom or toadstool is usually all that can be seen of the fungus. The bulk of it consists of an extensive network of minute tubes (the mycelium) which spread through the host, whether this be tree, leaf, soil or dead wood.

In addition to the ground-living species many types of fungi grow attached to a tree trunk or stump, these are bracket fungi and some of the most prominent occur on old birch trees. Around this area there are some spectacular examples, some of which run all the way up old stumps like fairy steps to heaven.

Go straight ahead at the crossroads until a large clearing is reached then take the right-hand path downhill through the wood. Turn left at the wide path.

A rest on the bench at the crossroads provides the opportunity to take in the ancient feel of this woodland, named Pool Hollies. The park's woods consist mainly of oak, holly and birch and cover about a quarter of its area, principally in this north-eastern corner. Many other species are present, nearly all planted, although willow and rowan together with the heath-invading birch will establish themselves from seed. The association of oak, rowan and holly is a notable feature of the woodland ecology. Elm, ash, and hawthorn are all rare within the park.

The characteristic under-shrub in the woods is holly which grows in remarkable abundance and contributes to the darkness of many of the copses. It is one of those species that bears male and female flowers on separate plants – a fact that explains those mysterious hollies with which some gardeners persevere for years without ever getting any berries for Christmas. The familiar prickles of the leaves are missing from the foliage at the top of the trees, these higher leaves having a smooth oval outline. The reason is that the prickles have evolved as a defence against browsing animals, so it is safe to assume that if giraffes or koala bears lived in this country the prickles would go all the way up! Nature being the variable thing that it is, a number of hollies will be found with smooth leaves right down to the lowest branches. Smooth or prickly, look out for the yellowish blotches which betray the presence of a mining maggot of the phytomyza fly which eats the leaf from the inside, thus avoiding the points anyway.

Insects and other mini-beasts thrive in the benign conditions found in Sutton Park as a result of it never having been extensively used for agriculture, and thereby avoiding the worst of the depredations caused by habitat loss and chemical spraying. This is typified by the continuing presence of the holly blue butterfly whose somewhat peculiar life style is easily accommodated here. As its name implies this butterfly's preferred food plant is holly, although in spring females will lay their eggs on a variety of other plants including dogwood, spindle, alder buckthorn and gorse. The yellow-green caterpillar feeds on buds, flowers and developing fruit before pupating slung beneath a leaf. In August the second generation is on the wing and this time the females are far more fastidious in their choice of food plant upon which to lay their eggs. They always choose the flower buds of ivy, into which the young larvae burrow head first. As ivy flowers very late – from September to November – the butterfly's strategy allows it to take full advantage of a late source of protein in the growing cells of the ivy flowers before nodding off for the winter in its silken bivouac.

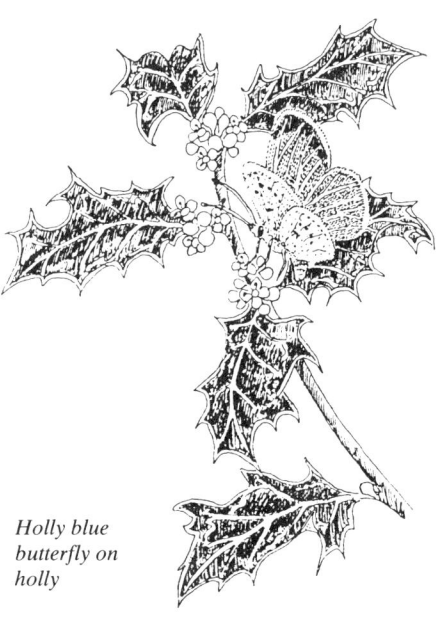

Holly blue butterfly on holly

In late summer the paths are sprinkled with scarlet rowan berries, and plantains thrive in the trampled edges. Exotic trees such as larch, Corsican pine, sweet chestnut and red oak will all be found, some in 'plantation order', others growing more casually. The difference between the regimented rows of a confier plantation and the tangled kaleidoscope of semi-natural woodland can be clearly seen on either side of the path. On the left a big old rowan stands guardian over a patch of green-stemmed bilberry, the bright leaves of which make it very prominent. More often encountered on heaths and moors, bilberry is also a plant of acid woodland when the canopy is open enough to let sufficient light through. This leads it to favour path and ride edges, and small clearings. Its common and scientific names – bilberry and *Vaccinium myrtillus* – bring together two different strands of our history. The Latin-derived 'vaccinium' may well be a corruption of the Latin word for a berry, 'baccinium', whilst the name 'bilberry' comes from the Danish 'bollebar' meaning 'dark berry'.

Turn right at the fork and almost immediately right again to go down to the pool. Follow the pool edge round to the right and over the plank bridges.

Just before Bracebridge Pool is reached a short straight path to the right leads to the 'Druid's Well', a spring around which a stone shelter was constructed in about 1815. It is named more for fancy than for fact and all that now remains of the shelter are some mossy stones surrounding a rectangular trough.

The water's edge brings a brush with civilisation at the adjacent restaurant and refreshment kiosk. They continue a long tradition as they are on the site of a Tudor hunting lodge where, no doubt, noble hunters paused to quaff ale and nibble cold venison. If Henry VIII did hunt in the area he may have stood on this very spot enjoying what many consider to be the most beautiful view in the park. One commentator was moved to declare this was one of the loveliest scenes in England. Perhaps for him these lines by Rudyard Kipling would be appropriate:

The Sutton Rose – The red rose of Sutton's coat-of-arms is reputed to commemorate the saving of Henry VIII's life by a local girl when a wild boar attacked him in the Park. Amongst his gifts to her was a red rose.

*God gave all men all earth to love,
But, since our hearts are small,
Ordained for each one spot should prove
Beloved over all;*

*That, as He watched creation's birth,
So we, in godlike mood,
May of our love create our earth
And see that it is good.*

From *Sussex*, a poem by Rudyard Kipling

Certainly the beauty of this landscape is remarkable considering how very close it is to a major centre of commerce and industry. The little island posing so artistically is a reminder that it is a combination of man and nature that has produced it.

Bracebridge Pool has substantial populations of swan and painter's mussels as well as freshwater snails. Of the five sorts of freshwater mussels found in Britain the swan mussel is the largest with specimens known to reach nine inches in length. The smaller painter's mussel can be up to six inches long. Both species burrow into mud in large ponds, lakes and canals.

Painter's mussel

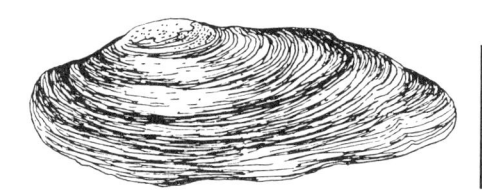

Painter's mussel – Early Dutch painters found the shells of this species ideal for holding their colours, hence its popular name.

Striding over the little bridges, accompanied by the music of many hidden birds, the walker seems to be in a woodland version of medieval ridge and furrow farmland. The furrows are drainage channels built to improve conditions for the trees, although some erosion now seems to be taking place as a result of encouraging the water to run away. In places exposed networks of roots make it look as if the trees are desperately clinging on to handfuls of soil. On a smaller scale the sides of the furrows are festooned with bright green miniature hanging gardens formed by liverworts. These are primitive plants which, like the mosses they are related to, are very simple and reproduce by spores rather than seeds. They are typically found in moist, but not permanently wet, places.

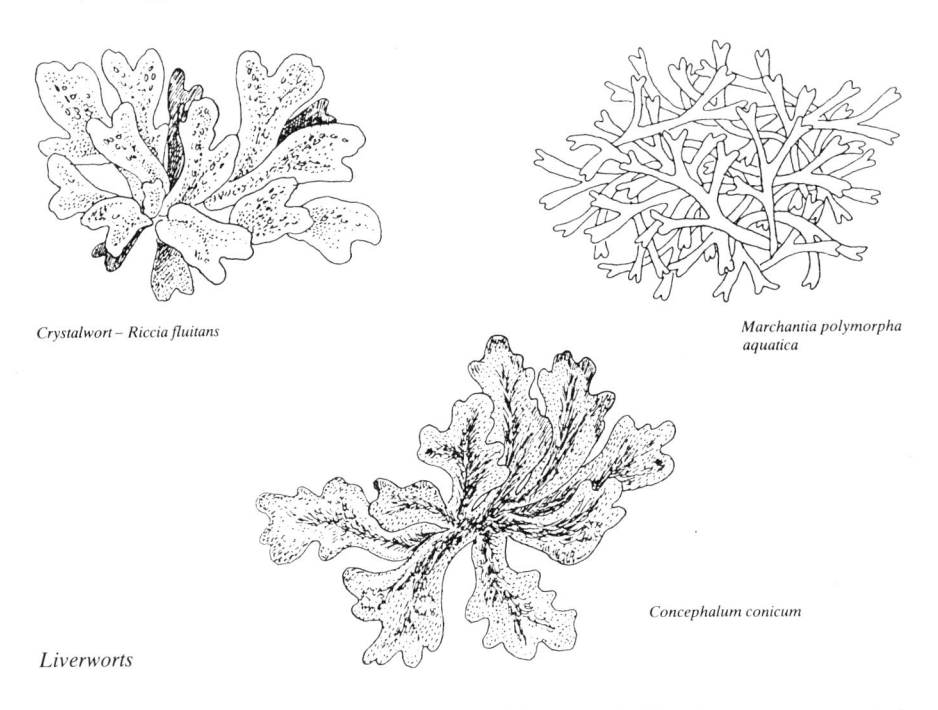

Crystalwort – Riccia fluitans

Marchantia polymorpha aquatica

Concephalum conicum

Liverworts

Where a wide path comes down from the right, turn half-right over a concreted pipe and follow the path. The next junction is an ill-defined jumble of ways through the trees. Pick a way to the left eventually meeting the well-defined path that was used on the outward part of the walk. Turn left here to return to the small pool. Proceed back over the little bridge and take the right-hand fork to go under the railway. Bear left between the pines and the birches to the wide track and turn left to the starting point.

Bracebridge Pool was probably built as a fish-breeding pool in the 15th century to supply fresh bream to the manor. It seems likely that Little Bracebridge Pool was a 'fish-stew' – a secondary pool to which fish were transferred for final fattening before being eaten. The stream which feeds it is called the Ebrook, but downstream it becomes Plants Brook and flows into the reservoirs of that name

Snipe

Butterwort

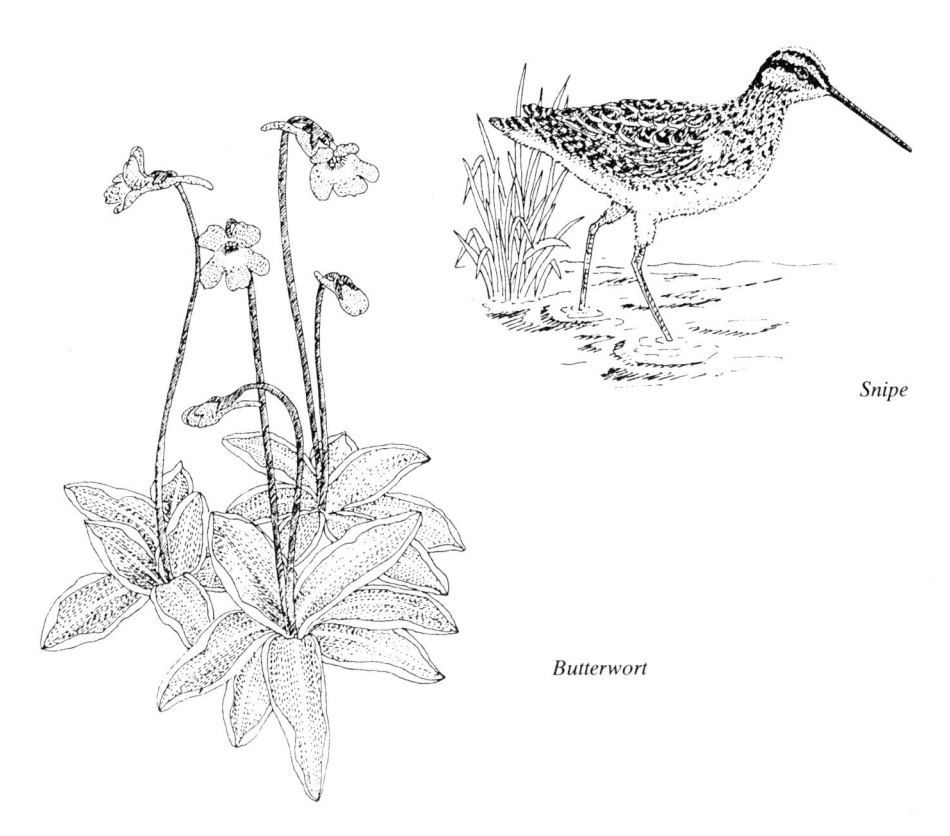

featured elsewhere in this book. Around its banks to the right of the path are a series of acid bogs in which grow a number of the park's rarities. Orchids, sundews, louseworts, ragged robins, sneezeworts and marsh thistles – each delight the eye in their season. Snipe, lapwing and heron are safe in the seclusion provided by the muddy bogs which protect them from human disturbance.

One of the prettiest bog flowers in June and July is common butterwort, their solitary violet flowers nodding at the top of their leafless stalks. The plant can be spotted at any time of the year because of its bright yellow-green rosette of thick leaves with rolled edges. Like the sundews, butterworts supplement the meagre diet supplied by their roots by trapping insects on their sticky leaves and then rolling the leaves inwards to digest them.

Emerging from the arch a complete change of scenery is discovered. Instead of the woodlands and wetlands, the third major habitat of the park – heathland – presents itself. Purple heather and occasional flecks of yellow gorse can be seen in front of the distant Streetly Wood which spills young birch over the heath. This illustrates one of the main problems in conserving the heathlands which are everywhere being invaded in this way. Some marsh thistle has found its way across the railway and the grass is spangled with golden flowers of tormentil, its four petals distinguishing it from the rest of the genus *Potentilla* which have five.

The heathlands are home to the emperor moth, a handsome creature with eye-spots on each of its four wings. The smaller males are day-flying and are equipped with feathery feelers which serve to detect the scent of the more sedentary females. It is the only British member of the mainly tropical Saturnidae family which includes the enormous atlas and moon moths.

As the track is reached another 'natural' horizon is seen at the top of the rising ground ahead; grass, gorse, and trees filling the view. The grass is noticeably different on the slope because crops were grown here during the last war. Although this was for a relatively short time the land was agriculturally improved. It now provides a striking example of how even a temporary change of land-use can cause a permanent change in natural features, short-term gain having to be set against long-term loss.

Emperor moth on heather

PLANTS BROOK

Photo: Cathy Wells

The raised wooden boardwalk enables the walker to reach right into the wet woodland and reedswamp

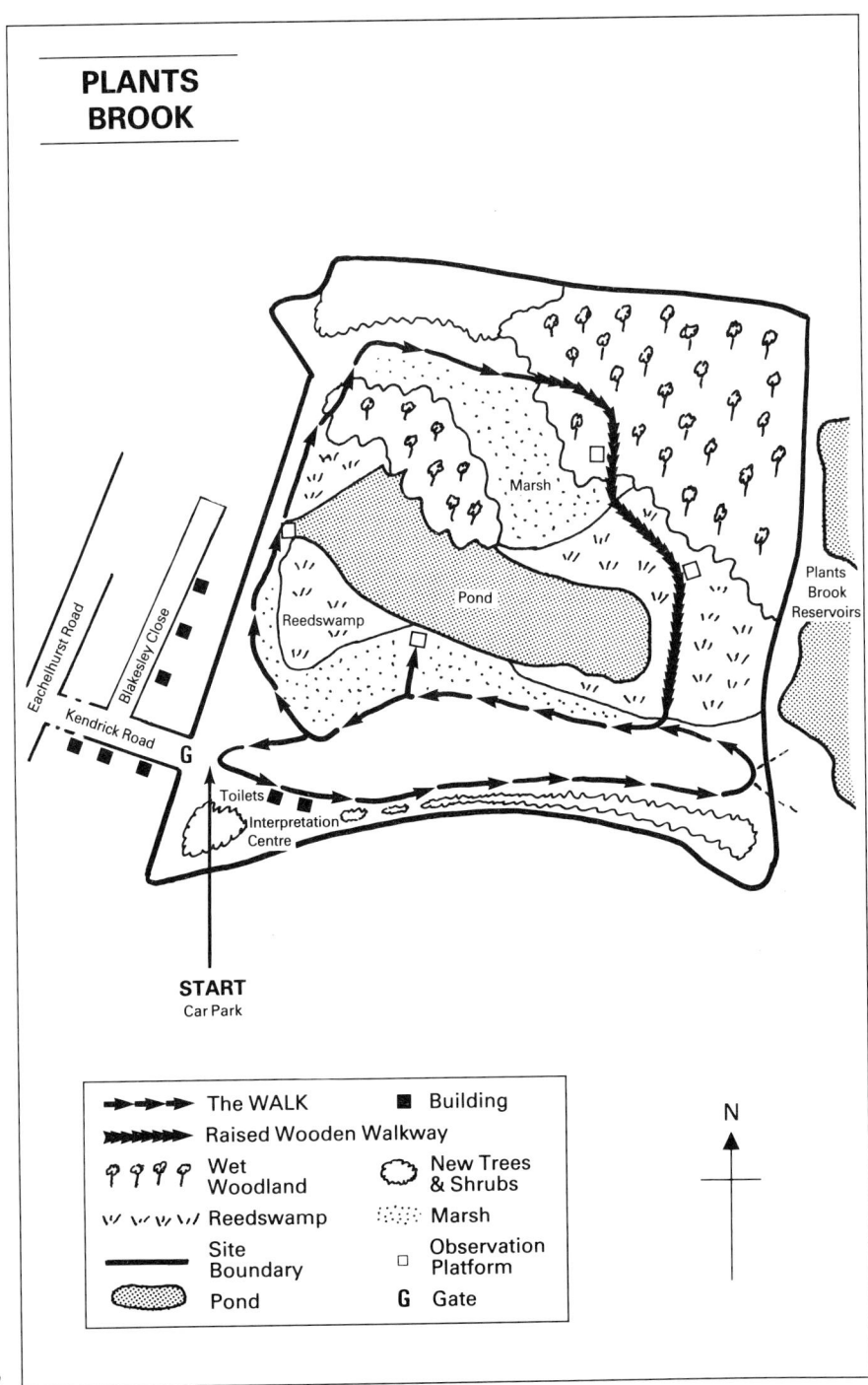

PLANTS BROOK

START Car Park

Legend:
- ➤➤➤ The WALK
- ➤➤➤ Raised Wooden Walkway
- ♀♀♀♀ Wet Woodland
- \\/ \\/ \\/ Reedswamp
- —— Site Boundary
- Pond
- ■ Building
- New Trees & Shrubs
- Marsh
- ▢ Observation Platform
- **G** Gate

N

42

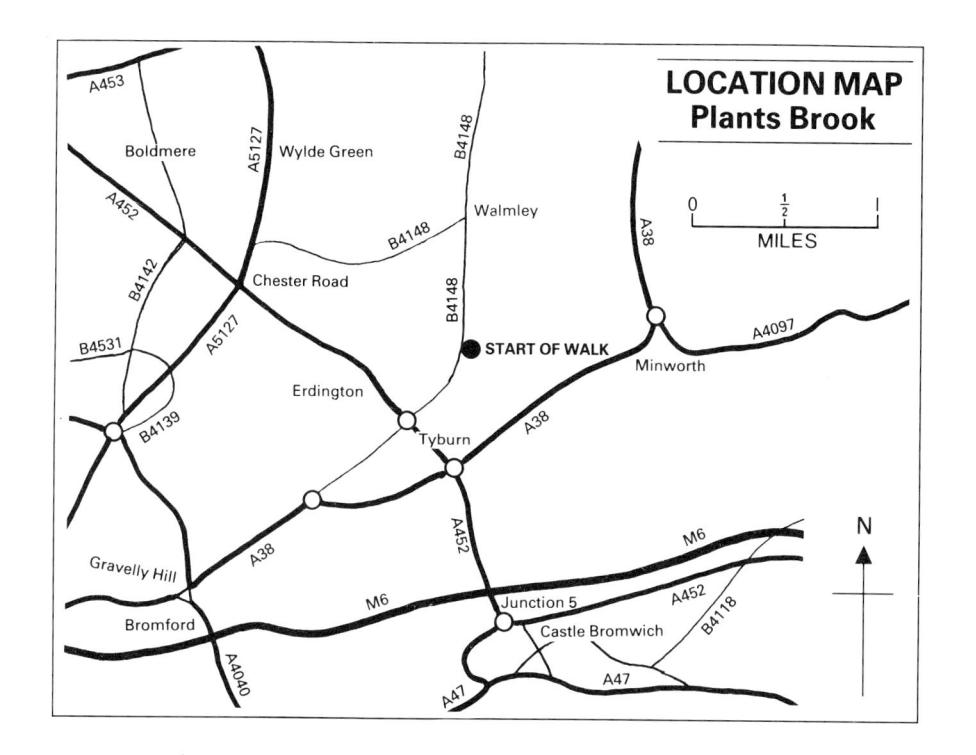

PLANTS BROOK

O.S. SP19 (1:25000) – 137921   Approx. ¾ mile

An easy, flat walk on well-made paths around a pool partly surrounded by woodland.

Plants Brook Community Nature Park occupies nine acres out of a total of 30 acres of pools and woods marking the site, five miles from Birmingham city centre, of the last drinking-water reservoirs built in the city, in 1860. The still unpolluted water is particularly rich in invertebrates which in turn support a varied population of birds, such as water rail and dabchick. When David Bellamy officially opened the nature park in July 1985 he enthused over the rich variety of plants, birds and insects living there.

Park in Kendrick Road or, if the gate is open, in the small car park in the reserve. Alternative parking is available at nearby Pype Hayes Park. If parking in the road please take care not to block residents' driveways or make undue noise – the nature park always wants to be a good neighbour.

Start from the warden's office, where information will be available about current wildlife activity. At the time of writing a new enlarged centre is being planned that will be sited nearer to the large pool. Walk towards this pool, with the meadow on the left and the new hedge on the right.

On a fresh cool spring morning, perhaps following overnight rain with a turbulent sky promising more to come, an intermittent sun sparkling now and then on the distant water, and a brisk wind making the tall trees roar louder than the birds can sing, the air at Plants Brook could only be described as bracing. But it is far from the sea, nestling in the suburbs between Birmingham and Sutton Coldfield with a distant tower block standing sentinel-like over it. This tiny jewel of a place is literally a living testimony of the efforts of those local people who had to fight in the late 1970s and early 1980s to prevent the area being used for tipping. They fought to have its wildlife value recognised, implemented a management plan to protect and enhance that value, and today remain vigilant in the face of continuing threats from the formal water-sports lobby to make more intensive use of the water.

Looking now at the buttercups, clovers and plantains crowding around the new plantings of rowan, guelder rose, oak and ash, watching the wood-pigeons wheeling about the tops of the mature trees, or the starlings (now safe from merlins which preyed upon them in winter) peacefully probing the mysterious menu of the meadow, it is difficult to conceive how anyone could even think about destroying such a treasure. That 'bracing' wind will urge that shelter should be sought in the wooded area, where this poem may be reflected upon.

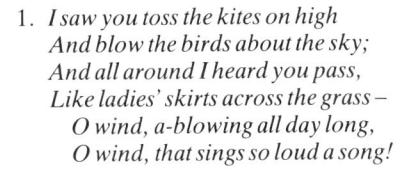

Merlin

1. *I saw you toss the kites on high*
   And blow the birds about the sky;
   And all around I heard you pass,
   Like ladies' skirts across the grass –
   O wind, a-blowing all day long,
   O wind, that sings so loud a song!

2. *I saw the different things you did,*
   But always you yourself you hid.
   I felt you push, I heard you call,
   I could not see yourself at all –
   O wind, a-blowing all day long,
   O wind, that sings so loud a song!

3. *O you that are so strong and cold,*
   O blower are you young or old?
   Are you a beast of field and tree,
   Or just a stronger child than me?
   O wind, a-blowing all day long,
   O wind, that sings so loud a song!

The Wind, by Robert Louis Stevenson

Make a U-turn and follow the path along the opposite edge of the meadow back towards the gate.

Look for the mugwort and wormwood growing here. These are closely-related members of the daisy family, although this is not immediately obvious to the untrained eye. They are tall aromatic herbs with small flowers, not at all like their showy cousins, and can easily be told apart by crushing the leaves, wormwood having a much more powerful smell than mugwort. Up to the beginning of this century wormwood was considered scarce but it has since found conditions to its liking, at least in the towns of the Midlands. It can now be found, as here, on many bare sites, alongside roads and paths.

> *Wormwood's scientific name of* Artemisia absinthium *gives a clue as to its popularity in France. The potent drink of absinth is made from this herb. It is also commonly used as an ingredient in vermouth.*

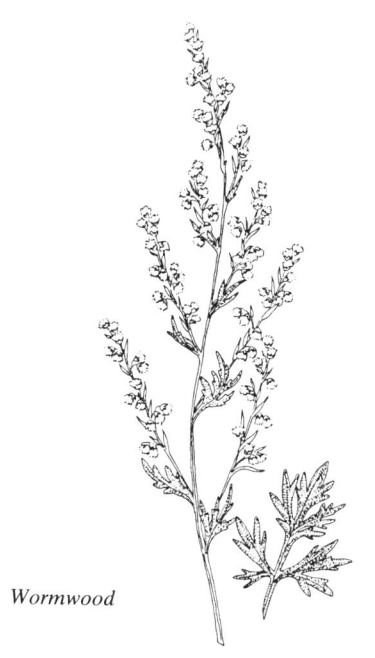

Wormwood

Also growing between this path and the pool are orchids – one of the most popular attractions of Plants Brook. It is a matter of some curiosity as to why some members of the plant and animal kingdoms have what seems to be a disproportionate appeal. Frogs seem to be all right (potential princes perhaps?) but not snakes; squirrels but not rats; swallows but not magpies. Orchids certainly possess a magic aura, so making their presence always noteworthy. Maybe it is their centuries-old reputation as aphrodisiacs, or the fantastic forms their flowers take, or even their exotic connections which single them out. It is salutary to recall that they had a very mundane use in some parts of the world where their roots were dried and powdered to be used as a beverage before coffee became universally available. Would their aura have survived if our high streets contained 'orchid houses' and the Italians had invented the 'Espresso orchid' machine!

> *Orchid seeds will not germinate properly, if at all, without the presence in the soil of a particular fungi called* Mycorrhiza. *This makes them a very difficult group to cultivate.*

Southern marsh orchid

Here there is a very good population of southern marsh orchids. The flowering spikes form prominent stands in the grass from June to July, varying in colour from pale pink to bright magenta, and having unspotted leaves. Orchids are notorious for hybridising, thereby disguising themselves as closely-related species, which leads to much debate amongst botanists as to exactly what species may have just been found. At least the time spent by the specialists arguing the finer points of taxonomy can be used by the more casual observer, who may be accompanying them, to appreciate the flower's beauty.

Take the short path on the right to the wooden platform.

This platform is not used for angling from – that is not allowed here. But it is an ideal place for pond-dipping, returning items found to the water, and watching for signs of the rich mini-beast population living in the pool. Frogs, toads and newts all breed on the site. Newt tadpoles are easy to separate from those of the frog or toad as they have feathery gills, and are usually to be seen from late spring to midsummer. Unlike the other two they are carnivorous from the moment they hatch, feeding on small crustaceans like daphnia or cyclops. Do not spend time looking for 'newtspawn' – there isn't any. Females lay their eggs singly, attaching them to plants and stones.

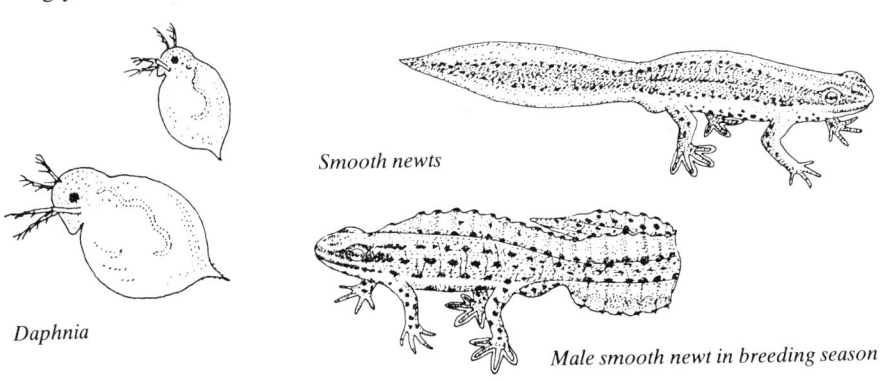

Smooth newts

Daphnia

Male smooth newt in breeding season

Other aquatic creatures include the nymphs of various insects such as dragonflies, damselflies and mayflies. These are the immature stages of some of the most beautiful insects we have, with their bright metallic-greens, reds, and blues. Each group is quite distinctive: dragonfly nymphs are heavily built, relatively short but stout creatures without really prominent appendages except for their six legs; damselfly nymphs are long and slender, often bright green with long antennae and three feathery 'tails' which are actually gills; mayfly numphs not only have three similar 'tails' which may be straight or feathery, but also a row of gills along each side of the abdomen. It is sometimes possible to sit here and watch the wonderful sight of a great cloud of mayflies shimmering over the water as if in a silent insect discotheque. The dancers are all males, hoping to attract female partners. Adult mayflies do not feed and so their emergence from the water, after perhaps three years as nymphs, has to be synchronised so that mating can take place immediately, and the eggs laid during the adult's brief lifespan.

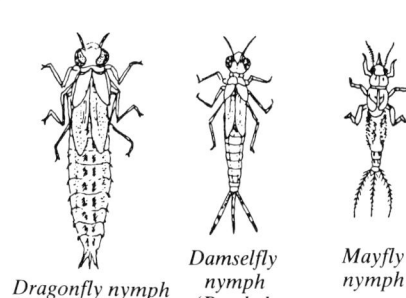

Dragonfly nymph (Hawker)   *Damselfly nymph (Banded demoiselle)*   *Mayfly nymph*

> *Dragonfly nymphs possess highly modified jaws, unique in the insect world, which shoot out, propelled by hydraulic pressure, to capture prey. The accuracy with which this device is used implies an ability to estimate three-dimensional space.*

Another denizen of the area is the water spider. Of all the thousands of different species of spiders in the world this is the only one to live almost permanently under water. A number of others are associated with wet places such as pond margins and bogs but they are not able to live below the surface. The water spider spins a silken bell in the water and supplies it with air from the surface, so making a kind of submarine within which this fundamentally terrestrial creature can live a dry but submerged existence. The only time in their lives that they voluntarily leave their watery lairs is as young spiders when they rise to the surface, spin a filament of silk to catch the breeze, and balloon away on the off chance of coming down near, or in, another stretch of water. This is the exact opposite of the countless humans who, in different places and at different times, have left their homelands and islands to take their chances in frail rafts set adrift at the whim of tides and currents on mighty oceans. How many of them found a good landfall, and how many of these little spiders find a good 'waterfall'? Not being satisfied with one distinction in being the only water-dwelling spider in the world, this species claims another in that, unlike other spiders, the males are generally bigger than the females.

Retrace the steps to the path and turn right. Just before the gate turn right again and follow the path around the pool and over the boardwalk.

From late spring look out for the scrambling tendrils and purplish flowers of common vetch, and the bright-yellow four-petalled flowers of greater celandine. The latter will be found flowering all the way through from April to October. Chewing the root of greater celandine used to be recommended as a cure for toothache – maybe just another old wives' tale but there could be some truth in it. Despite the name it is not a member of the buttercup family; it is in fact a sort of poppy, and as poppies are the source of opiates then this plant may well have pain-relieving properties.

Greater celandine

During summer the pool may be covered in a foreign water fern known as Azolla. The unauthorised introduction of this plant has caused considerable management problems. This demonstrates just how sensitive sites like this are to such thoughtless actions.

At any moment the peace and tranquility of this corner may be shattered by a watery commotion as two or three of those most aggressive birds – coots – try to settle a territorial or mating dispute in their own inimitable fashion. They rear up, wings flapping wildly as if grappling for support in the water behind, and, with heads back, they kick at each other before losing the uneven battle with gravity and flopping back down into the water. Like wary boxers they then circle cautiously before repeating the exercise.

Meanwhile, only a few yards away, another pair of coots will be engaged in peaceful attendance to their young. Unlike their parents these fluffy grey chicks have a bright-pink face, which is permanently pointed to one of the parents, looking for the next tit-bit. Coots feed mainly on vegetable matter, which is a different diet to the great crested grebe, dabchick (little grebe) and water rail with which they share Plants Brook. The dutiful parents can be spotted with assorted pieces of damp salad drooping from their bills heading for the voracious chicks.

A number of plants from different families have evolved a climbing habit and three of them are present in the Community Nature Park. White bryony is

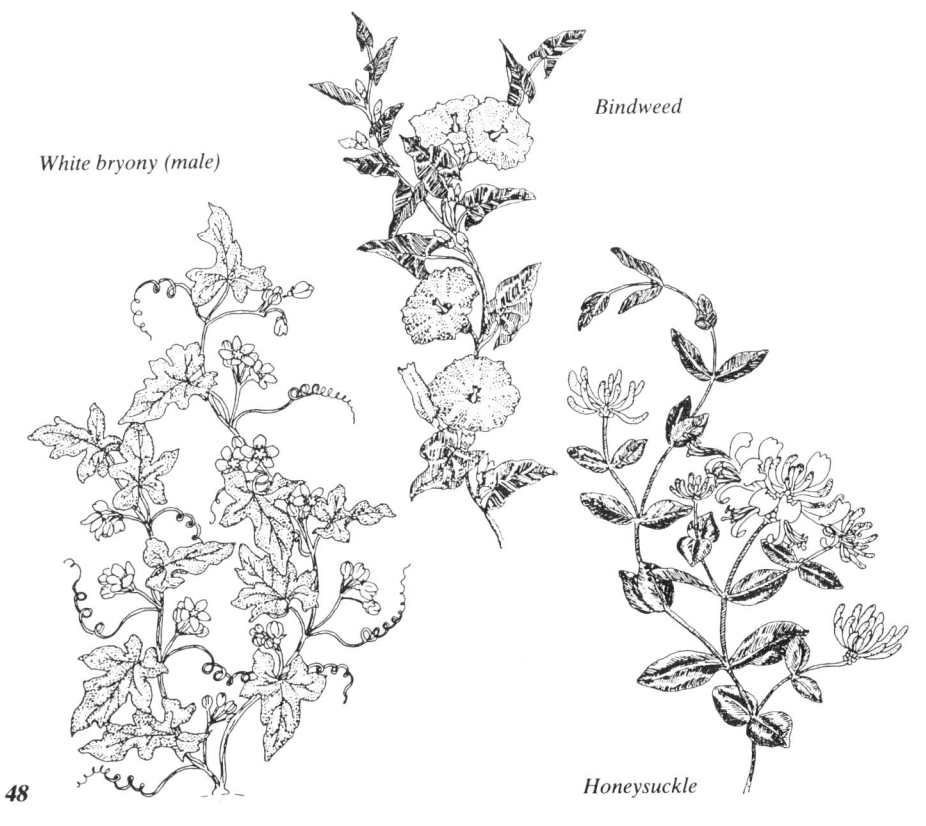

Bindweed

White bryony (male)

Honeysuckle

the only member of the gourd family which grows wild in Britain. It is not related to black bryony, although, coincidentally, that is also the lone representative of its family in this country – the yams. White bryony will twine its way up to four metres high, and a casual glance could write it off as ivy as the leaves have a similar shape. Closer inspection reveals that opposite the leaf stalks are coiled spring-like tendrils which support the plant. The five-petalled greenish-white flowers appear in late summer. The second climber is hedge bindweed, a plant which will creep, if there is nothing to climb up, for about three metres. It has arrow-shaped leaves and large trumpet-like white or pink flowers. These flowers are much favoured by the large bumble-bees which lumber in and out of them, no doubt thinking they have found the 'horn of plenty'. Favourites with bees they may be but not with gardeners as bindweed is one of the most pernicious of all garden weeds, obstinately resisting all efforts of eradication. At Plants Brook its attractions can be enjoyed without any problems. The third member of this triumvirate is honeysuckle, the only climbing member of its family, which includes the wayfaring tree, guelder rose and elder. Sometimes a pest to foresters because of the damage it can do to young trees – hence its alternative name of woodbine – the showy flowers, gentle scent and midwinter green provided by its young leaves, make it one of the most popular of our wild plants. It is most scented at dusk when the moths which visit its flowers are just up and about. Strangely, honeysuckle always twines clockwise whilst bindweed always grows anti-clockwise. This led Flanders and Swann to pen the famous song *The Bindweed and the Honeysuckle,* relating the sad tale of parental opposition to a mixed marriage, their objection being based solely on the criterion of which is the correct way to climb.

As the boardwalk is approached a wild bouquet presents itself, including red campion, buttercups, Queen Anne's lace, germander speedwell, ground ivy and white dead-nettle. A pause on one of the boardwalk seats will give the opportunity to soak up the atmosphere of this hidden corner of suburbia. The very trees make music here as the rhythm of the wind in their crowns acts as a counterpoint to the notes made by boughs meeting overhead across a path and 'singing' as they rub together, as if to imitate the birds. The feathered fraternity contains blackbirds, mistle thrushes, wrens, reed buntings, collared doves and kingfishers. Whether feeding, singing, nesting or preening they provide a constant backdrop of colour, movement and music. From the second seat it is possible on a still day to look down, rather than up, at the treetops as they are clearly mirrored in the water beneath.

Kingfisher

Depending on the season the marsh over which the boardwalk is built will be wetter or drier, but it will always be the way into the area of greatest diversity in the reserve – brim-full of plants, animals and birds. Quiet pedestrians have the best chance of seeing one of Plants Brook's most charming citizens, the water vole. These harmless vegetarians are often wrongly called water rats, besides they are altogether more 'cuddly' than any rat. They are rounder and have much flatter faces and small ears. Water voles are often active during the day and if disturbed at the water's edge they make a quick dive beneath the surface. Often the first indication of their presence is the single splash heard as they enter the water. They then swim directly away from the bank, underwater, leaving a telltale trail of bubbles above. Not so happy in the water but very much at home above it are the bats, who take over the insect patrol at dusk from the swallows, swifts and martins, and whose acrobatic displays are a free added attraction on any summer's day. This poem captures their spirit.

Water vole

All day – when early morning shone
With every dewdrop its own dawn
And when cockchafers were abroad
Hurtling like missiles that had lost their road –

The Swallows twisting here and there
Round unseen corners of the air
Upstream and down so quickly passed
I wondered that their shadows flew as fast.

They steeple-chased over the bridge
And dropped down to a drowning midge
Sharing the river with the fish,
Although the air itself was their chief dish.

Blue-winged snowballs! until they turned
And then with ruddy breasts they burned;
All in one instant everywhere,
Jugglers with their own bodies in the air.

The Swallow, by Andrew Young

The second half of the boardwalk takes the path through a stand of lesser pond sedge. Sedges are a grass-like family of plants with triangular stems. The genus *Carex* to which lesser pond sedge belongs has the male flowers separate to, and above, the female flowers. Amongst the sedges grow false bulrush (reedmace), the beautifully aromatic water mint and celery-leaved buttercups. Above them all flit male reed buntings with black heads, white collars and chestnut bodies, accompanied by dragonflies and damselflies weaving their bright tapestries, whilst deep in the wood a willow warbler's cadence descends once again.

Reedmace has been called 'false bulrush' since the appearance of a popular Victorian painting named Moses in the Bulrushes *in which the artist depicted reedmace, not bulrushes, on his canvas. The true bulrush is a member of the sedge family.*

At the end of the boardwalk turn right along either side of the meadow to return to the gate.

GREAT BARR – URBAN SAFARI

The Tame Valley Canal

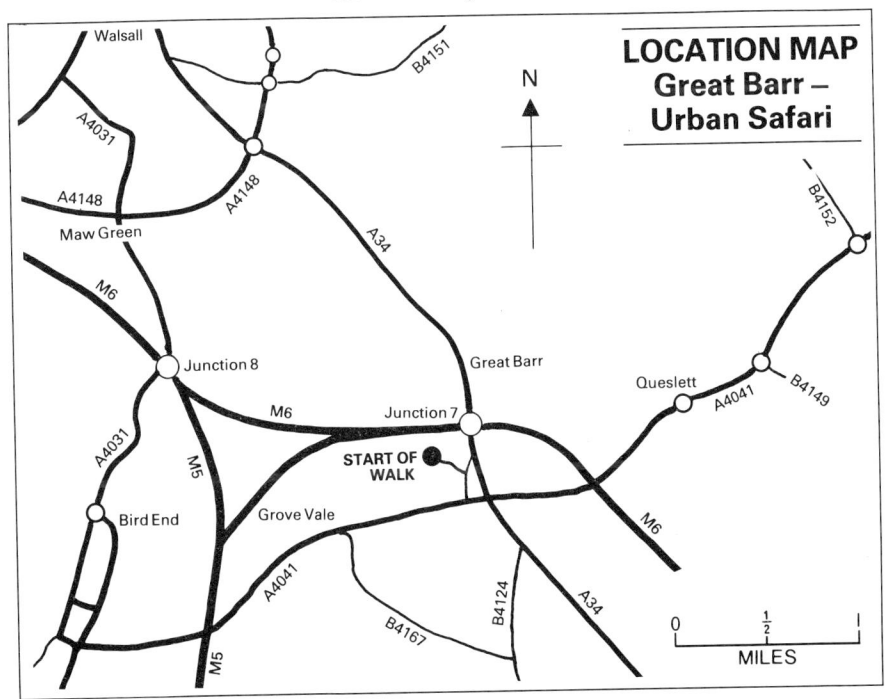

**LOCATION MAP
Great Barr –
Urban Safari**

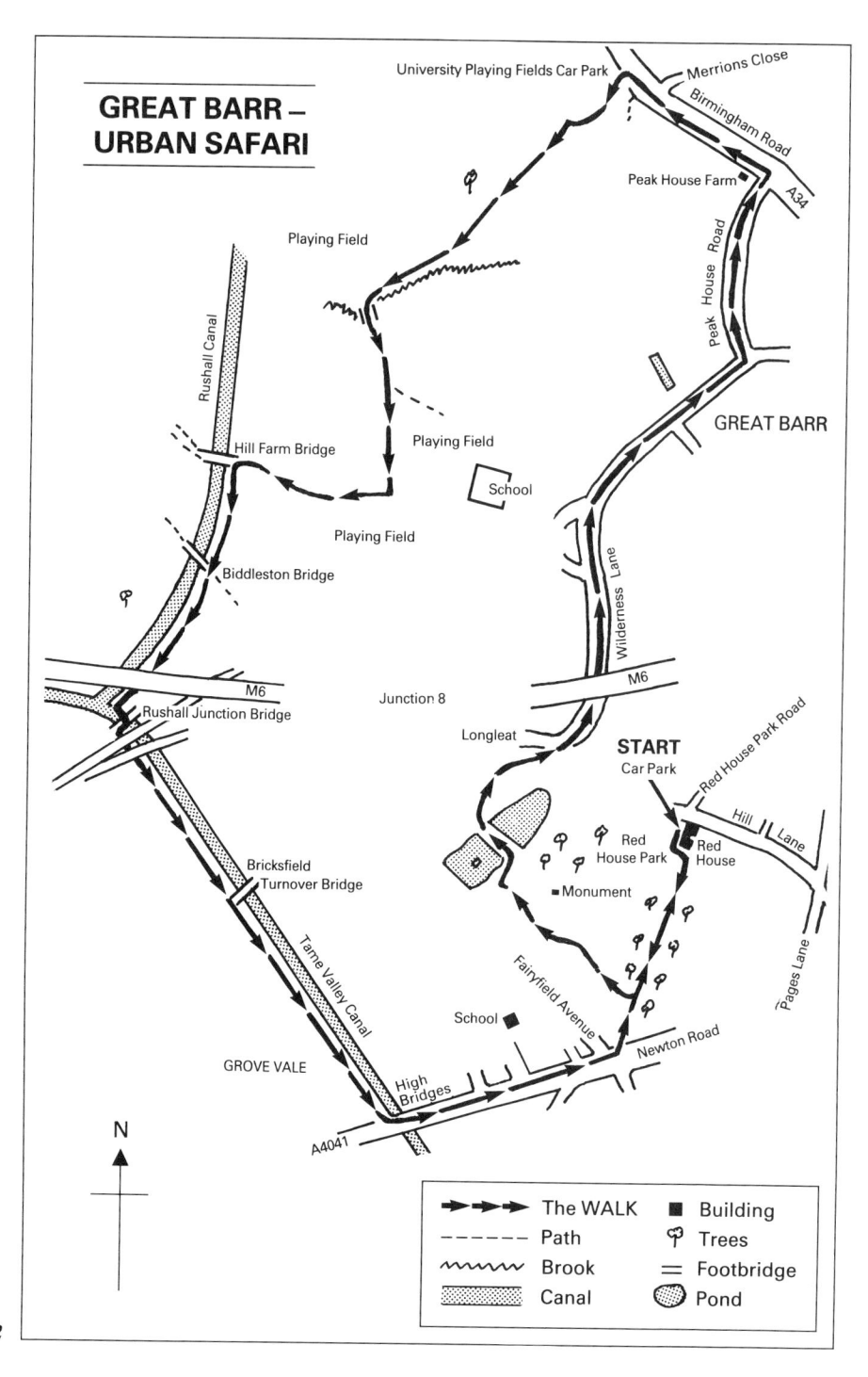

GREAT BARR – URBAN SAFARI

GREAT BARR – URBAN SAFARI

O.S. SP09 (1:25000) – 040945　　　　　　　　　　Approx. 3 miles

Discover the hidden wildlife of suburbia in this undulating but easy walk around part of the Great Barr area on the borders of Birmingham, Walsall and Sandwell.

The intensive development of the past two centuries has obscured the series of gently rolling hills and wide flat valleys upon which the 'endless village' of the Black Country was built. This walk takes in the ridge of one of these hills forming the eastern side of the Tame Valley. It allows good views of Rowley Hill in the middle of the Black Country, and Clent Hills which mark the return to open country to the west. The route takes in a Victorian town park, a fragment of forgotten woodland, an old farm, old hedgerows and pastures. A peaceful stretch of canal completes a surprisingly rich walk.

From the car park in Hill Lane, walk into Red House Park and past the old house ('Red House') with the formal rosebeds to the right. Turn right to pass beneath the avenue of limes and turn right again near the end of the path by the private gardens to go down the hill. Turn left where the pale cobbles appear and almost immediately right along an unmetalled path with the first pool on the left. Turn left and go between the pools. Follow the second pool round to the right and make for Wilderness Lane to go beneath the motorway bridge.

Red House Park is a typical Victorian town park complete with formal flower beds, acres of closely-mown grass, mature specimen trees, and uninspired modern tree planting. One of the real characters of the park is a tough old mulberry tree which leans at the corner of the main path by the house. Thousands of miles from its home in West Asia, with its orange and grey bark fissured and flaked, a steel band holding it together, fire damaged, and beetle infested, it still flowers and fruits as if to defy everything an insensitive world can do to it.

Leaving the mulberry tree behind, the path goes through an imposing avenue of limes – stately trees well suited to such a position where they can grow unchecked, in contrast to the sorry specimens, so often found in streets, which have to be lopped and hacked about because they grow too big. These trees are common limes, hybrids between the small- and the large-leaved limes. By midsummer they take on a lovely yellow-green hue as thousands of star-shaped flowers open. All the local bumble-bees come to dance attendance upon them so that every tree is alive with sound, movement and colour.

On the bank to the right of the path going down the hill is a curious assemblage of young trees, with aliens such as sycamore, Turkey oak, red oak, Norway spruce and horse chestnut having been planted alongside native species like beech, ash, sessile oak, alder and mountain ash. The whole group has a rather sad air, somehow contriving to be neither formal nor informal; utilitarian nor ornamental, grudgingly living together when each would be better suited to different companions in other places.　　*53*

> The common lime is Britain's tallest broad-leaved tree, a specimen in Yorkshire reaching a height of 46 metres (150 feet). Limes are the Linden trees of many folk songs.

Lime foliage and flowers

Both pools have the usual hard edges found in parks, ideal for feeding the birds from in winter but not so good when it comes to the breeding season. The older pool on the left is reasonably well sheltered as well as having an overgrown island, and is generally favoured by the birds in summer over the newer, somewhat sterile, pool on the right. That ubiquitous urban quartet – mallard, moorhen, coot and Canada goose – all somehow manage to raise their flotillas of fluffy chicks here. The strange flowers of common figwort will be found on the left of the path: an odd-looking plant which numbers amongst its close relatives flowers as diverse as snapdragons, foxgloves, mulleins and speedwells. Further on to the right there is a patch of chicory, sometimes called succory. A sort of dandelion, this is surely one of our most beautiful wild flowers, the stemless blossoms being a wonderful lilac-blue with white pollen-tipped dark-blue stamens. Not the usual Parks Department flower but nice to see even so.

Chicory

Just after passing beneath the motorway and opposite the school, make a detour into the enchanting sliver of wet woodland to the right of the footpath. This patch of woodland, scrub and grassland, nestling between motorway and houses, covers about ten acres and is typical of many such forgotten corners of suburbia. It is home to many flowers, trees, birds and insects, a link with the rural past and a hope for a more sympathetic future. Dark reflections through the trees reveal the presence of shallow pools. In summer they are black with tadpoles, shivering and quivering as ten thousand tiny tails propel their owners in an unceasing quest for food. Some of them become food themselves for vor-

Family of Canada geese

acious dragonfly nymphs for whom an unending diet of tadpoles never seems to pall. Above them, marsh cinquefoil and yellow flag bloom whilst young oak and hawthorn scrabble skywards, the gaunt fingers of a dead tree pointing the way. An adult dragonfly, a brown hawker, patrols his territory around the tree like a miniature bi-plane and from deep in a thicket a tiny wren pours out its rich song. A miniature snowstorm seems to be in progress around one of the oak trees which closer inspection shows to be a horde of small moths. These are oak tortrix moths, pale green above but almost white beneath. Delicate and ephemeral their aerial ballet is but a prelude to the appearance of cohorts of caterpillars which live inside rolled-up oak leaves and chomp away at them non-stop. Their single-minded attention to the task in hand frequently results in the almost complete defoliation of the trees concerned.

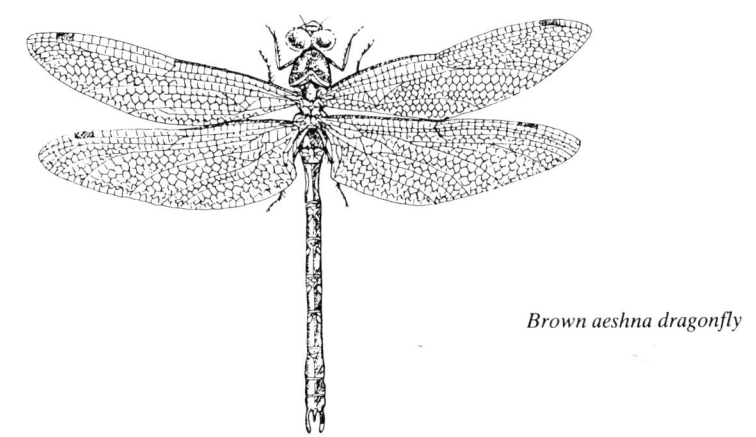

Brown aeshna dragonfly

A slightly unnerving experience one may have here is to hear the click-click-click of a bicycle being wheeled over the field, to stop apparently right behind the walker, who on turning round, finds nothing there! The culprit will be one of the hundreds of grasshoppers hiding in the grass and 'singing' either to attract a mate or warn off potential rivals. To a lady grasshopper it may be sweet serenading but to human ears it sounds just like a bike, and to the hovering kestrel it probably sounds as if supper is singing for itself.

Cross the road to turn left into Peakhouse Road. Turn left again at the main road and walk down the hill until the University playing fields car park is reached on the left. Enter here and find the 'Beacon Way' signs. Follow them around the edge of the playing fields, behind the school, over the metal footbridge, eventually to reach the Tame Valley Canal.

Peakhouse Farm, on the corner of the main road, may not now be as busy as in earlier times but chickens still run free in the yard and a venerable old barn survives the ravages of time with a fringe of ragwort beneath its hat of tiles. A solid Georgian farmhouse faces the busy traffic on the main Birmingham to Walsall road, no doubt disregarded by many of the high-speed commuters that pass it every day and who remain unaware of this historical corner. Peakhouse is well named, sitting as it does on a high ridge looking out over the Tame Valley. Just past the house, before the start of the hedge, a view opens up to the Clent Hills on the Worcestershire side of the West Midlands. The hedge on the left of the footpath sits on a bank, partly supported by an old drystone wall. It is fairly tall now but the horizontal branches at its base are evidence that it was once laid, a stockproof barrier which would have prevented any animals on the other side from getting under the wheels of the carts and carriages which once passed this way. Wild flowers fairly tumble out of it: mugwort, hogweed and hedge garlic in one place, hedge woundwort, brambles and woody nightshade in another. The last named, also called bittersweet, climbs through the hawthorn to appear above head-height with its bright-purple petals surrounding yellow anthers. The nightshades are all members of a generally poisonous family *(Solanaceae)* which nevertheless provides two of our most widespread foods: tomatoes and potatoes. The berries of bittersweet which go from green to yellow to brilliant red are indeed poisonous. Just before the car park the main hedgerow plant changes from hawthorn to blackthorn.

Woody nightshade

Herbalists used woody nightshade as a cure for vertigo, but not in pill or potion form. Their prescription required that it be tied around the neck.

After skirting the car park the landscape to the right changes from playing fields to rough herbage, back to playing fields and then to hay fields, whilst on the left is a beautiful old hedge. Now tall and unlaid it has enough variety of woody species to suggest it could be very old, if not ancient. In places forming a double hedge over a deep ditch, it contains oak, ash, willow, wych elm, English elm, elder, hazel, sycamore, wild rose, field maple and hawthorn. The herbaceous plants include black bryony, woody nightshade and great willow-herb. Many of the trees are now so large that the hedge is more like a narrow strip of woodland. In comparison to the average hawthorn hedge this a rich ribbon of foliage winding across the fields. What a harvest of nuts, berries and seeds must be here for the taking each autumn, and what an assortment of mini-beasts must lurk and skulk amongst the leaves and branches. For fur, feather and feeler alike the hedge is a combination of motorway, restaurant and high-class housing. The author of this poem would have been quite at home here writing these lines:

> *Now summer is in flower and nature's hum*
> *Is never silent round her sultry bloom*
> *Insects as small as dust are never done*
> *Wie glittering dance and reeling in the sun*
> *And green wood fly and blossom-haunting bee*
> *Are never weary of their melody*
> *Round field hedge now flowers in full glory twine*
> *Large bindweed bells wild hop and streak'd woodbine*
> *That lift athirst their slender throated flowers*
> *Agape for dew falls and for honey showers.*

From *The Shepherd's Calendar*, by John Clare

A few hundred years ago two seeds escaped the notice of would-be diners and dropped by a ditch to germinate and grow into tall trees, flowering and fruiting in their turn before falling (or were they pushed) to lie alongside the path. These huge bulks of timber appear to be solid and immovable but they are slowly being consumed by a range of organisms including fungi, beetles and woodlice. So called 'dead' timber is really full of life, acting as a sort of natural battery that has spent many years being charged with energy which is now very slowly being released. Instead of calling these bustling colonies 'dead trees' perhaps they should be thought of as bundles of sunbeams collected over previous years to give life to so many plants and animals today. A particularly attractive fungus which grows on them here is oyster fungus. This spectacular toadstool produces masses of grey-blue fruiting bodies and is more usually seen on living trees, especially beech.

Oyster fungus

As the blocks of flats are approached spend a few minutes leaning over the five-bar gate on the right of the path – whether or not a straw is chewed in country yokel style is entirely optional! Survey the peaceful scene in front: flats to the left and the low school buildings away to the right there may be, both half hidden by greenery, but in front is a field of grasses and clovers, and all around are those fabulous hedgerows punctuated with mature trees. Depending on the time of year, there could be an accompaniment of birdsong or the humming of insects. It requires some effort to recall that this bucolic setting is about half way, and in a direct line, between the centres of Birmingham and Walsall. Turning away from the gate, a colourful corner is revealed where white hogweed, mauve-pink rosebay willowherb and bright-yellow perfoliate St. John's wort delight the eye.

On any warm summer's day the paths and fields will play host to any number of brown butterflies. The orange-brown moth-like, almost triangular ones are small skippers, the males of which are distinguished by a dark line of scent scales across the fore-wings. A lighter-coloured butterfly with a dark spot in the corner of each fore-wing is the small heath, Britain's most common and widespread butterfly. More numerous around here than either of these two is the larger meadow brown. This is dark brown and has orange eye-spots on each fore-wing. Their habit of flying up at the last minute makes them seem to appear from the toes of your shoes. Flying is almost too strong a word to describe their floppy progress as they half-heartedly flap across the tops of the grasses for just a few feet before landing again. Meadow browns usually breed in the same field as their parents, thus showing a marked lack of the wanderlust that others of their kind, such as clouded yellows and red admirals, display by their long migrations across Europe. Each of the three species mentioned feed as caterpillars on grass, the meadow browns camouflaging themselves by adopting the same shade of green as the particular grass they are feeding upon.

The thin, relatively poor soil along this part of the route is strewn with many different sorts of flowers and even a cursory examination reveals that many of them are members of the pea family. With white and red clover, yellow bird's-foot trefoil, meadow vetchling, and purple tufted vetch it is easy to forget that, as well as being very attractive, the pea family (*Leguminosae*) is probably second only to the grass family in economic importance to man. With about 17,000 species worldwide it is not surprising that we should find a use for some of them. Many varieties of peas and beans are eaten, indigo dye, gum-arabic and gum-tragacanth are obtained from others; some produce timber, others (clovers, sainfoins and Lucernes) are utilised as fodder, whilst laburnum and wisteria decorate our gardens. There is a fanciful link between the butterflies and the plants they flit over in that all the native British legumes are in the subfamily *Papilionatae* ('papilio' being Latin for butterfly). It is so-called because of a supposed resemblance of the flowers to butterflies, perhaps not immediately obvious but a wonderful excuse for lingering and looking at the blossoms.

> *Because of their protein richness lentils were widely eaten by Catholics during Lent, giving rise to their name. In turn the shape of lentils caused the word 'lens' to be used for curved pieces of glass.*

Where the path passes above the canal a search of the field to the left should be rewarded with the discovery of two wild gentians. One of them – common centaury – is not rare but it does have a delicate beauty with its fresh green leaves and bright-pink, five-petalled flowers in umbel-like heads. The other is more unusual as it is normally found in limestone areas. It is yellow-wort, noted as having grown on Silurian limestone a few miles away in the vicinity of Dudley in 1801.

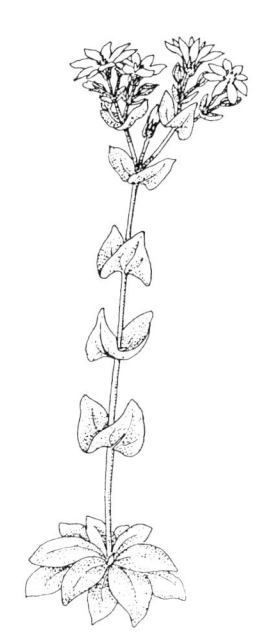

Yellow-wort

At the junction of the canals turn left and almost immediately right over the bridge. Do NOT follow the 'Beacon Way' signs which point straight ahead but turn left along the canal towpath. After some way, just before the high road bridge, take a right fork and go up the embankment. Pass through the small gate on to the pavement and turn left over the bridge. Walk on to the park gates on the left, turn into the park and return beneath the avenue of limes to the Red House and the car park.

This deep, cool, shady cutting, filled with birdsong, lined with luxuriant vegetation and buzzing with insect life provides a complete change of atmosphere to the open landscapes around Peakhouse Farm. The focus now is on things close to: tench and roach engage in the age-old battle of wits with anglers, pond-skaters and whirligig beetles dance dervish-like on the surface of the water, and shoals of tadpoles roam like miniature watery wildebeest. The tangled herbage to the right of the path provides a perfect home for scorpionflies,

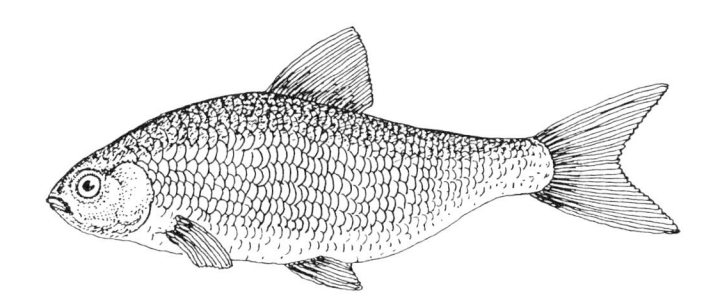

Roach

Scorpionflies   *Female*

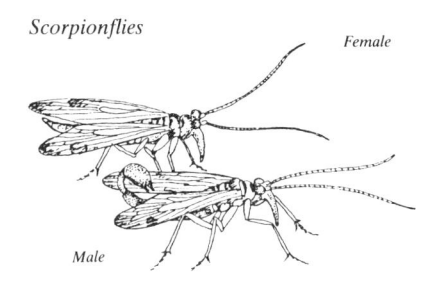

Some members of the small group of scorpionflies are little changed today from fossil forms over 250 million years old. They are the insect equivalent of the more famous coelacanth fish.

Male

insects that are neither scorpion nor fly! They belong to a small group which are quite unmistakable because of their long snout, four large wings with dark patches and, in the case of males, upturned reddish bulbous tails which give them their name. They are very much creatures of shady and damp hedgerows and banks.

The sudden transition at the little gate from peace and seclusion to noise and bustle is startling to say the least. Crossing the bridge soon aids recovery as it is realised that the highway authority has kindly built an aerial walkway through the tops of the tallest trees in the canal cutting. In winter squirrel-spotting is easy from here and, in summer, dusk brings out the pipistrelle bats from their roost in the concrete beams supporting the road. At any time it is quite an experience to look down into the trees instead of up as is usual; their shape, perspective and character are all completely changed. Passing back through the park our old friend the mulberry tree can be seen screening the Red House as it is approached beneath the limes. Lions, apes and elephants there may not have been, but our safari has had just as many curious and fascinating plants and animals as any in Africa.

Grey squirrel

MOSELEY BOG

Moseley Bog – a mixture of relic rural woodland and neglected Victoria gardens

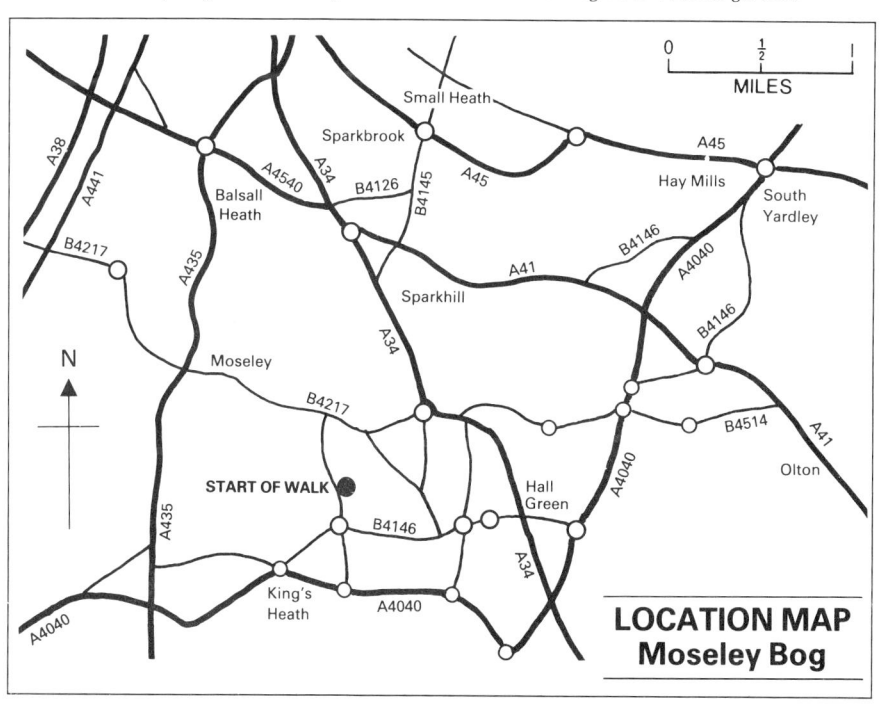

LOCATION MAP
Moseley Bog

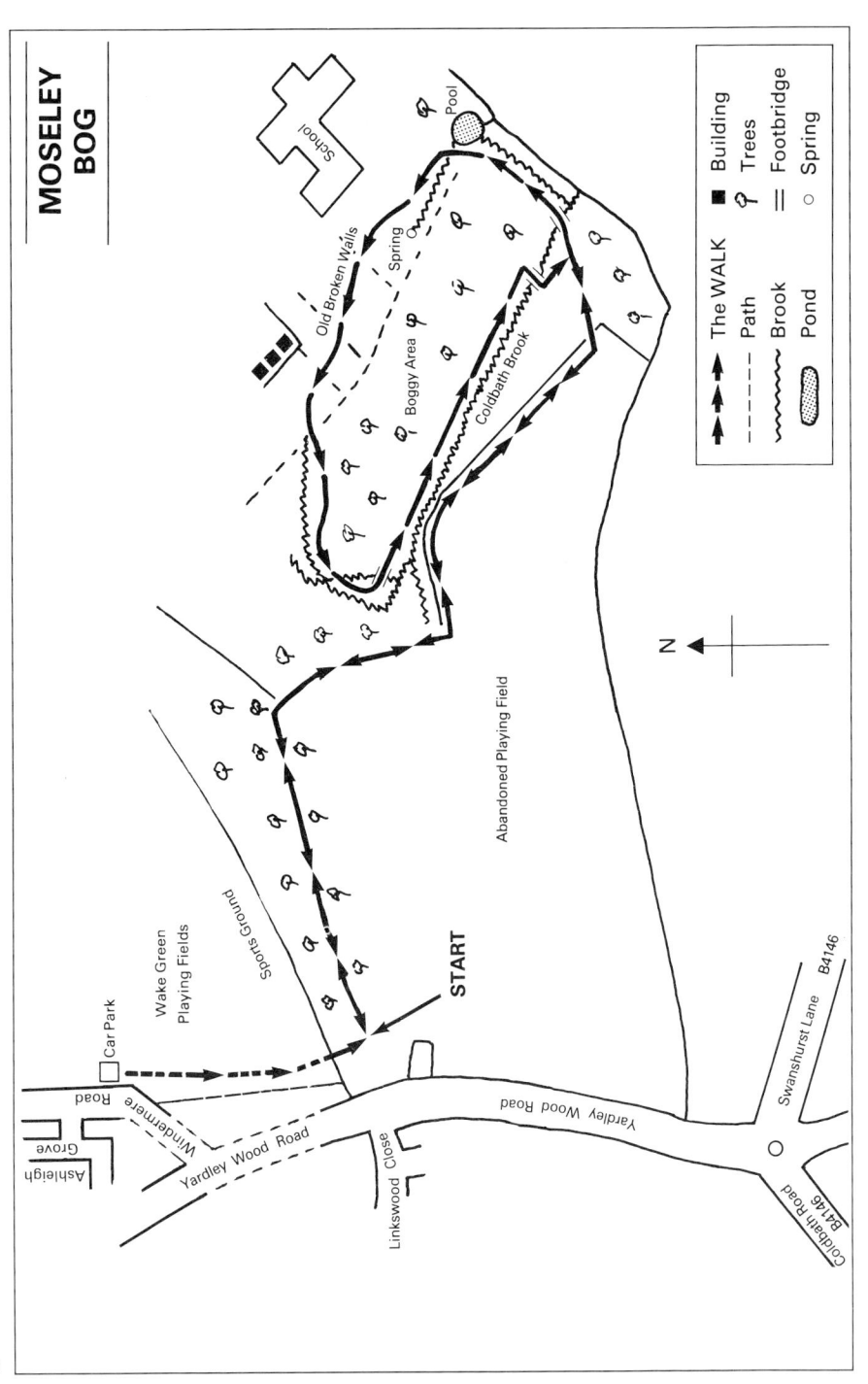

MOSELEY BOG

The WALK
- Path
- Brook
- Pond
- Building
- Trees
- Footbridge
- Spring

MOSELEY BOG

O.S. SP08 (1:25000) – 090821　　　　　　　　　　Approx. 1½ miles

A walk through wet woodland and neglected Victorian gardens. All easy going but can be very wet and muddy.

Moseley Bog is a fascinating site only three miles from Birmingham city centre. This magical, almost secret, place is home to a variety of wildlife which includes some uncommon plants. It was a boyhood haunt of J. R. R. Tolkien who lived nearby – but no hobbits have been recorded yet! A few years ago local residents saved the site from housing development with their 'Save Our Bog' campaign. It does not take long for visitors to be captivated by its charm.

Park in the car park in Windermere Road opposite Ashleigh Grove and walk across the playing fields to the entrance of Moseley Bog in Yardley Wood Road near to the junction with Swanshurst Lane and Coldbath Road. From here walk along the bottom of the bank on the left, between the beech trees.

Moseley Bog is a glorious tangle of wet woodland, covering about 14 acres, three miles to the south-east of Birmingham city centre. Nine acres are all that remain of a botanically famous area which included Greet Common and Moseley Wake, whilst the other five are the remnants of neglected Victorian gardens. The mixture of relic rural woodland and old gardens has produced an area of outstanding beauty, enchanting atmosphere, and unique conservation value. This combination has resulted in its designation as a Site of Special Scientific Interest (SSSI) by the Nature Conservancy Council, and as a Local Nature Reserve by Birmingham City Council. Although a visit at any time of the year is worthwhile, the details given here are based on what will be enjoyed in late February. Later in the year cuckoo flower, herb robert, guelder rose and feverfew join with many other flowers to create a colourful daytime banquet for butterflies such as the speckled wood, large skipper and meadow brown. At night their scents attract moths including the burnished brass, marbled minor and foxglove pug. For now the more muted shades of late winter bring their own charm.

The name Moseley Bog is somewhat misleading as the place barely belongs to Moseley (which thinks of itself as a village, albeit one that has been surrounded by an expanding city), and hardly has the character of a bog as the term is understood today. When a local was asked recently, 'Where is Moseley Bog?' the answer was, 'It's been in Yardley, Worcestershire. One map has Sparkhill written across it and recently it left Hall Green to go back to Moseley. To many of the older locals it is part of Springfield!' The wet woodland supports a much greater variety of plants than the word 'bog' suggests but there is no doubt that acid bog was present in the vicinity up to the first half of the 19th century when such plants as sundew, grass of parnassus, bog pimpernel, lousewort and sphagnum were recorded. Of these only sphagnum is still present.

63

The bank rising to the left of the path is the top of what used to be a small valley through which flowed Coldbath Brook. Looking across the abandoned playing fields, now planted with young trees, the opposite valley-side top will be seen. The land was infilled some years ago to provide football pitches but proved to be totally unsuitable because of poor drainage. These newly-planted trees are a poor recompense for the futile loss of the valley habitat.

At the old oak tree turn right and follow the hedgerow, keeping it to the left.
The old oaks here provide a home for a great variety of minibeasts and the larger creatures which feed upon them. Look back at the one which marks the right turn and it will be seen to have a relatively low crown from which a number of stout boughs are growing at different angles. In winter this gives the appearance of a set of antlers and, as it gets older and begins to lose some of the outer twigs, the tree will become what is called a 'stag-headed oak'.

The hedge here was planted in recent years by pupils of a local school and its buds of hawthorn, wild rose and oak are full to bursting in late winter. Along the base of the hedge those yellow heralds of spring, colt's-foot flowers, with their leafless fleshy stems, push through the dead entangling stems of last year's grasses. Flocks of a dozen or more dinner-jacketed magpies may been seen wheeling in and out of the treetops, whilst below them in the hedge blackbirds and robins, sometimes accompanied by rosy-coloured bullfinches, flit around. Meanwhile, in the field to the right, small parties of redwings and fieldfares often occur. These are handsome members of the thrush family which move south from Northern Europe and Scandinavia to

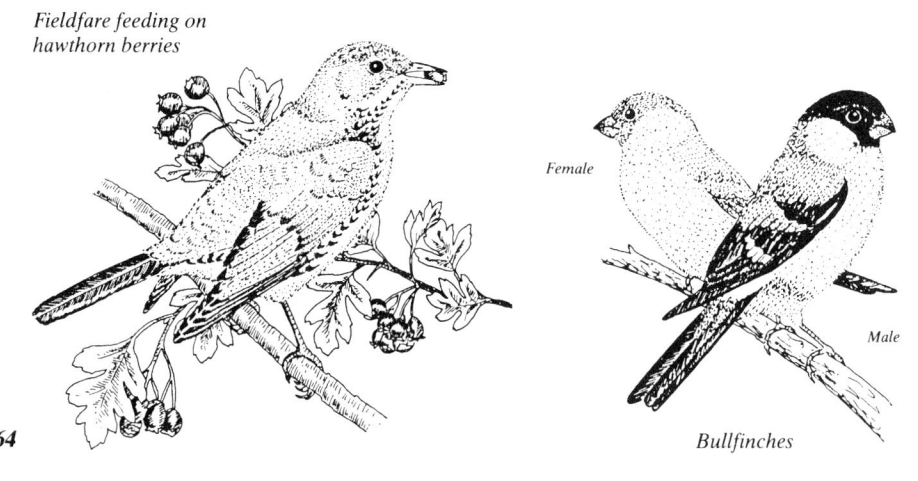

Colt's-foot flower stems

Fieldfare feeding on hawthorn berries

Female

Male

Bullfinches

winter in the British Isles. Both of them can be seen marauding along hedgerows, stripping them of haws and hips. When this food supply is exhausted they turn to the worms and grubs of pastures and fields.

Go down the bank to the left near the end of the hedge and follow the path over the footbridge and the fallen tree to the small pool which will be seen on the right.

Moseley Bog has an important literary association which not only enhances its reputation but also hints at its magical aura. J. R. R. Tolkien, author of *The Lord of the Rings* and *The Hobbit,* lived close by at 264 Wake Green Road from the ages of five to nine. This was at the turn of the century when the area was still considered to be in the country. Tolkien, whose vivid imagination would have been developing during this period, must have visited Moseley Bog frequently, and who knows which parts of it he later translated to 'Middle Earth', the imaginary world peopled with hobbits, orcs and ents. He is quoted as saying of this period in his life, 'Four years, but the longest and most formative of my life'. Perhaps this extract from one of Tolkien's poems says it all:

*I sit beside the fire and think
of all that I have seen,
of meadow flowers and butterflies
in summers that have been;*

*Of yellow leaves and gossamer
in autumns that there were,
with morning mist and silver sun
and wind upon my hair.*

*I sit beside the fire and think
of how the world will be
when winter comes without a spring
that I shall ever see.*

*For still there are so many things
that I have never seen!
in every wood in every spring
there is a different green.*

From 'The Fellowship of the Ring', *The Lord of the Rings,* by J. R. R. Tolkien

Where the path goes over the old dam look out, in late winter, for the pointed green leaves of bluebells pushing up through the brown leaf litter. Climb over the fallen tree which insists on producing a miniature forest of vertical shoots from its horizontal bole. The pool is not very big and at first sight it is just a damp corner covered in duckweed. From the middle of February to the end of March, however, it may be caught apparently boiling. Granted there will not be any vapour rising from it but the surface will be in a constant turbulence, with what will seem to be lots of bubbles breaking the surface. A closer inspection reveals that each 'bubble' is the head of one of a pair of mating frogs, dark on

Common frog

The common frog, the only frog native to Britain, is closely related to the toad and newt. Together the three groups comprise the British amphibians, represented by eight species, of which six are native.

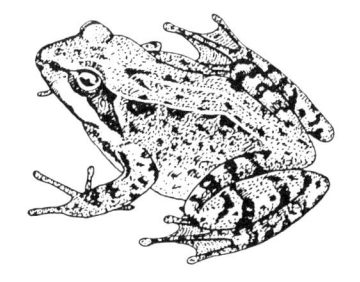

65

top with a pale bluey-grey throat. Over a hundred pairs may be found in this one tiny pond, demonstrating the importance of the place to the local survival of this amphibian. Although common here there has been a marked decline in the frog population in many parts of the country where it was once abundant, mainly caused by the filling in of ponds.

Step over the ditch and the fallen tree with its top in the pool. Turn left through a small area of holly, rhododendron and ivy. Follow the path to the right, away from the stream and behind the school buildings.

Even in winter the evergreens here combine to make a verdant bower, the native holly and ivy joining with that introduced member of the heather family, the rhododendron, to provide a contrast with the bare brown branches of the deciduous trees. Whilst passing through the patch of tall willowherb stems, each one terminating in a white wisp of downy seed, look for a pile of mossy logs to the right. Around here there is still some sphagnum moss growing. These mosses are genuine bog plants, communities of them dominate upland acid bogs in the north and west of Britain. In some places they are the only plants able to grow but here they struggle to maintain a foothold in an area of rich botanical diversity. Of the 14 species of sphagnum found in this country, ten will not tolerate any nutrient enrichment of their environment and each of them, having no roots, take all the sustenance they need from the rain which falls upon them – none can survive in running water. Most people are familiar with the use of sphagnums to line hanging baskets, a function which takes advantage of their capacity to absorb moisture to assist other plants to live in an arid situation. Perhaps it is not so well known that this same quality, combined with their gentle softness, led to their being used as field dressings in times of war. The small surviving patch here is a reminder of the range of bog plants which attracted those early Victorian naturalists.

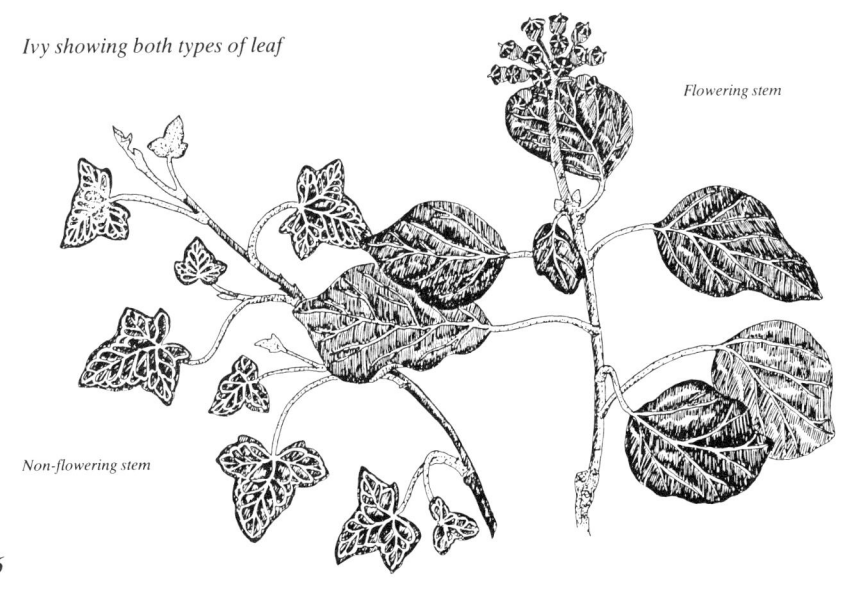

Ivy showing both types of leaf

Flowering stem

Non-flowering stem

The path twists and turns here. Keep the new houses to the right, turn left by the old lime tree, right through the old hedge and immediately left. At the ivy-covered spot, turn right, step over the fallen tree and make for the stream, turning left along its bank.

This section of the walk passes through the old abandoned gardens, as evidenced by the straight lines of leggy shrubs which mark their original boundaries. Not far from here grows one of the treasures of Moseley Bog – the royal fern. Noted as growing wild here two centuries ago but also known to be a popular Victorian garden plant, its presence provides a tantalising puzzle for today's botanists. Is the sole remaining specimen a relic from bygone days, or a 19th-century introduction, or a bit of both? Did some keen horticulturist find it by chance in his or her new garden and nurture it as an ornamental, so ensuring its survival for our enjoyment today? It is certainly rare in the wild in this part of the country – there have only been three recorded since 1901 in Staffordshire and it is too prominent to overlook. The royal fern is one of Europe's tallest, being capable of reaching a maximum of nine feet but more usually achieving about five feet. Its fronds resemble the leaves of higher plants. It is very distinctive in mid-summer when the centre fronds rise above the outer ones and produce golden-brown spore cases. At first glance it could be taken for a flowering plant at this time of the year.

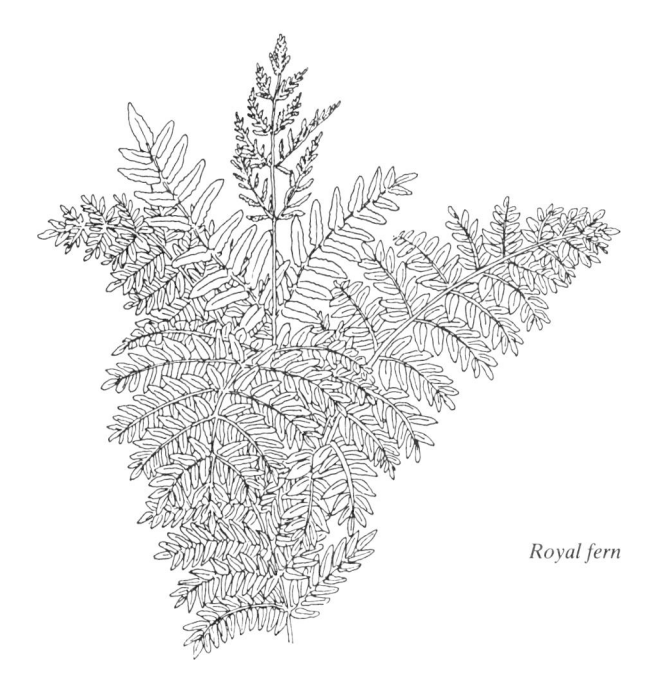

Royal fern

Another notable plant which grows here is the wood horsetail, a delicate and graceful relative of the troublesome common horsetails which are so difficult to eradicate from gardens. This characteristic plant of wet woodlands is chiefly found in Scotland, Northern Ireland and the North of England, and is not common in the Midlands. Horsetails are the descendants of the huge forest trees which grew in the tropical swamps of the upper carboniferous period (about 230 million years ago). The compressed remains of these giants formed the coal measures which provide so much of today's energy needs. It is fascinating to contemplate the miniature forest of wood horsetails in Moseley Bog and then think of their distant cousins forming a canopy 200 feet high all those millenia ago.

Horsetails are cone-bearing plants allied to ferns and look like miniature Christmas trees. There is now only one genus – Equisetum – but hundreds of millions of years ago they were a diverse and important group of plants.

Wood horsetail

Continue over the footbridge and stay on the left bank where the small stream joins a larger flow. Continue downstream.

The large stream is the curiously named Coldbath Brook. This watercourse is the original cause of the adjacent wet woods. Not far away is the restored Sarehole Mill which stands on the River Cole. Like most of the old mills in this region it relied on water for power and a drought constituted an energy crisis. To guard against this eventuality Coldbath Brook was dammed and the pool thus formed acted as an emergency water supply – a sort of hydraulic battery. It was named Old Pool, with first records of this name dating from 1781. Sometime about the middle of the 19th century, when the mill was converted to steam power and less water was needed, the dam was breached and the pool was drained. The resulting quagmire has developed over the past 120 years into the valuable woodland we enjoy today. Tolkien must have had a number of brushes with the miller because he is immortalised in one of his books as 'the white ogre', in contrast with a local farmer who became 'the black ogre'.

The brook rises about two miles away in Kings Heath, flows through the Bog and joins the River Cole at the mill. It presumably acquired this name because the water is always cold, which may be due to its fast flow and short length. Most watercourses flow faster and are shallower and colder nearer their source than elsewhere; as they progress they become deeper and slower and gain radiated heat from the land over which they pass. Coldbath Brook never has the chance to warm up in the two miles or so of its fall into the Cole, so it is probably very well named. There is evidence along its banks of the existence of a Bronze Age burnt mound site.

> *Burnt mounds are streamside concentrations of cracked, burnt stones dating from 3,000 years ago. At one time they were thought to indicate a cooking site. The lack of associated remains, such as bones, has led to speculation that they may have been primitive saunas.*

Walking on a carpet of oak leaves along the stream bank with the browns of last year's bracken and grasses contrasting with the dark-green holly and the 'old' green of bramble leaves, it is easy to forget that this enchanting fragment of Worcestershire countryside is now in the heart of Birmingham. The brown foliage clinging to young beech trees turns them into woodland beacons, reminding us not only of last year's growth but also of the brilliant green shoots which will soon be replacing them. The polka-dots of pussy willow show white against the dark bank. Soon the lumbering queen bumble-bees will wake from their hibernation to seek out the pollen-laden willow flowers which are an important source of nourishment for the early insects. The distant hum of traffic provides an almost gentle counterpoint to the 'teacher, teacher' call of a great tit, the soft rustle of the leaves adorning a young oak tree, the trickling of

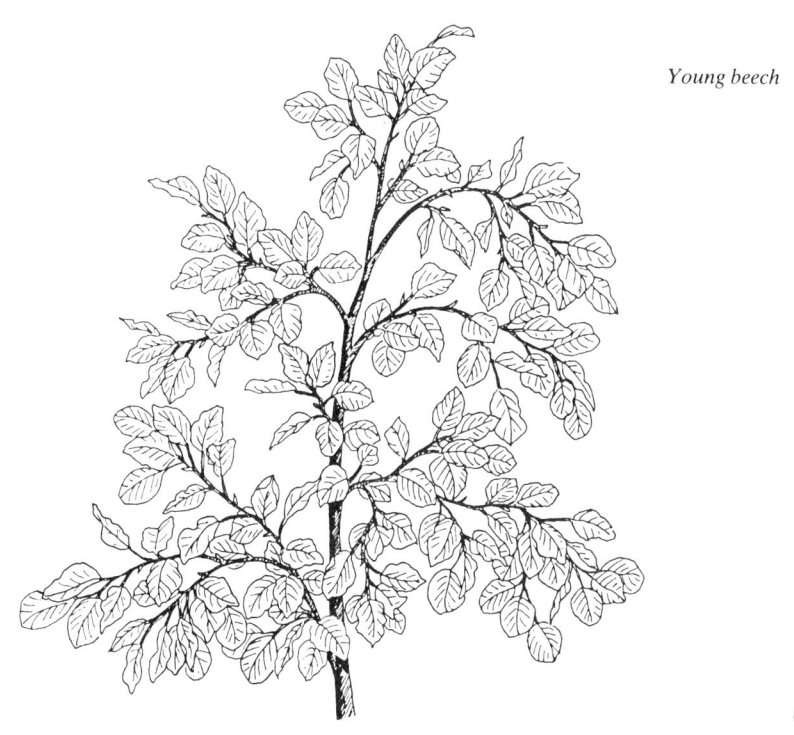

Young beech

the stream, and the drumming of a great spotted woodpecker. Pause where the tree has fallen across the brook and imagine that the writer of the following words must have known a very similar spot:

> On a warm, brilliant morning I paid a visit to a shallow pond which I had discovered some weeks before, hidden in a depression in the land. A group of ancient, gnarled and twisted alders grew just on the margin of the pond, and by-and-by I found a comfortable armchair on the lower stout horizontal branches overhanging the water, and on that seat I rested for a long time, enjoying the site of that rare unexpected loveliness.
>
> The chiff-chaff, the common warbler of the district was now abundant, two or three were flitting about in the alder leaves within a few feet of my head, and a dozen at least were singing within hearing, chiff-chaffing near and far, their note sounding strangely loud at that still, sequestered spot. Listening to that insistent sound I was reminded of Warde Fowler's words about the sweet season which brings new life and hope to men, and how a seal and sanction is put on it by that same small bird's clear resonant voice.
>
> Adapted from *The Return of the Chiff-Chaff*, by W. H. Hudson

Underfoot the dainty new leaves of Queen Anne's lace (cow parsley) seek the light whilst overhead a sparrowhawk may be seen or, more likely, black-headed gulls winging towards the mill pool at Sarehole Mill. Plump pigeons survey the scene as a grey squirrel scampers up a tree trunk. Here, in the heart of the city, nature has a stronghold.

Cross where the tree straddles Coldbath Brook and walk with the water to the left to regain the path coming down the bank from the right. Turn right retracing the route to the car park.

> In western lands beneath the Sun
>   the flowers may rise in Spring,
> the trees may bud, the waters run,
>   the merry finches sing.
>
> Or there maybe 'tis cloudless night
>   and swaying beeches bear
> the Elven-stars as jewels white
>   amid their branching hair.
>
> From 'The Return of the King', *The Lord of the Rings*, by J. R. R. Tolkien

Great spotted woodpecker

WOODGATE VALLEY

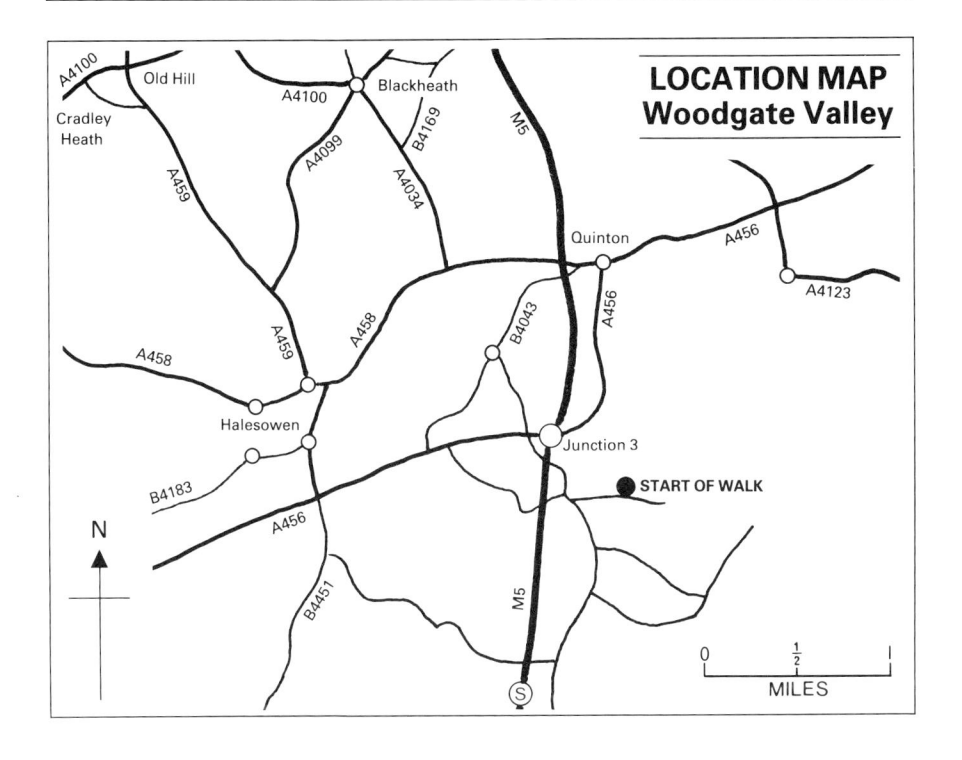

LOCATION MAP
Woodgate Valley

O.S. SO98 (1:25000) – 993829   Approx. 4 miles

A walk around the 'border country' where Birmingham and Worcestershire meet. The way is undulating though easy, but can be very muddy and wet where it passes through long grass.

Woodgate Valley, Bromwich Bluebell Wood and Bartley Green Reservoir each make their own special contribution to this route. Old farmland crisscrossed with hedgerows, flower-filled woodland, and exposed shoreline punctuated by water birds, provide ever-changing views in this remarkable corner of Birmingham. The proximity of the M5 motorway and the inclusion of some short stretches of street emphasise the intimate link between town and country, and serve as a reminder of how easily all of the natural features could have been lost. Not only has this not happened but the valley is now a country park with a modern visitor centre, financed by Birmingham City Council, and run by an enthusiastic and knowledgeable staff.

WOODGATE VALLEY

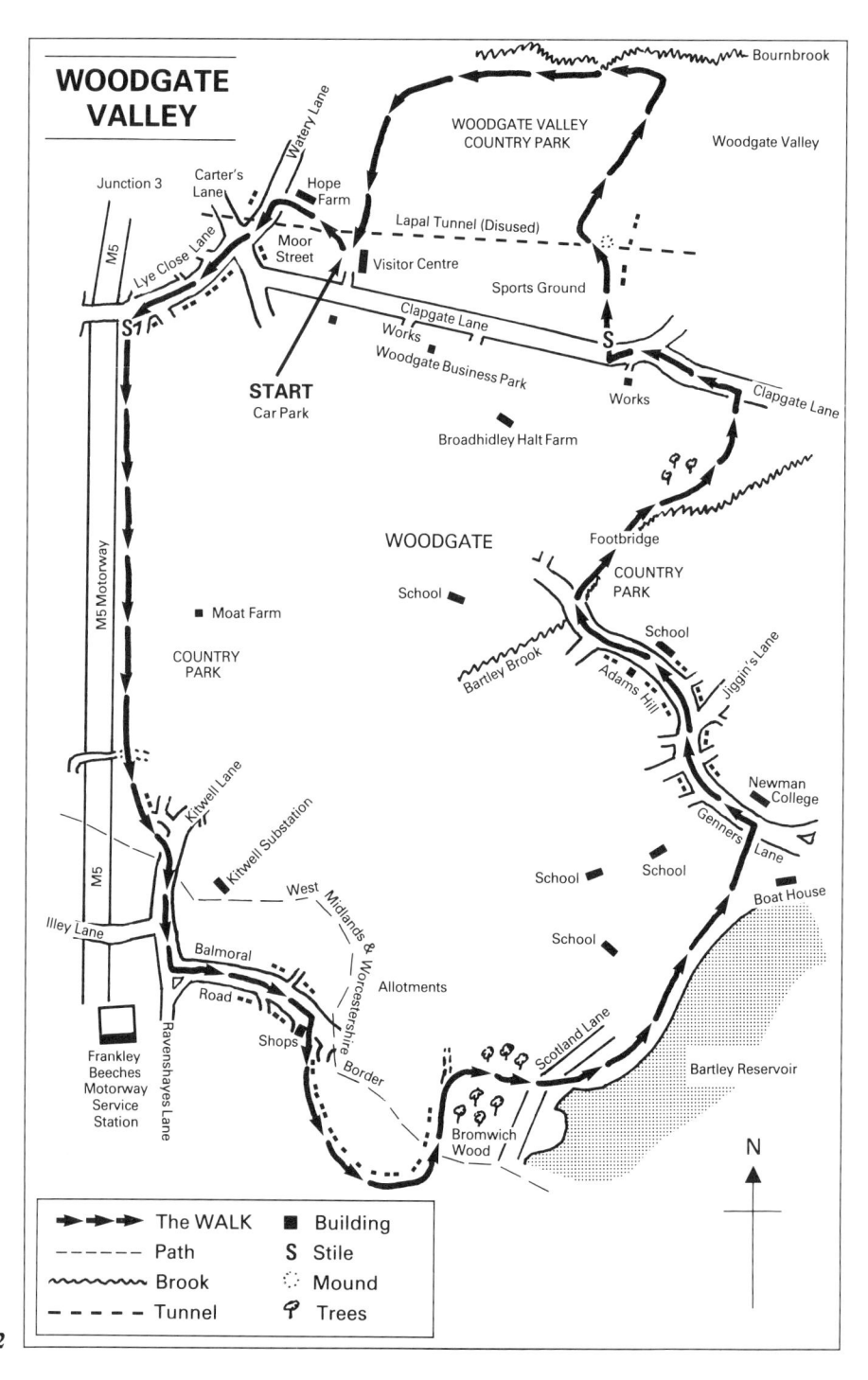

Park at the Visitor Centre in Clapgate Lane. Take the path past the car park which bends right then left to go through the farmyard. Turn left into the lane, cross the road and go down Lye Close Lane. Turn left over the stile above the motorway and pick your way across the meadows walking parallel with it until a road is reached.

Everywhere the Worcestershire countryside is reluctant to relinquish its grip on the woods and fields – housing, industry and schools nibble at, but never completely devour, this arm of the shire which reaches deep into the heart of the city. One of the farms in the area was called Wilderness Farm which may indicate the remoteness of the area in bygone days. There were plenty of other farms in the vicinity, including Stonehouse, Nonsuch and Four Dwellings. The present jumble of buildings at Hole Farm ranges from 18th-century barns to modern Portacabins and would probably not meet with the approval of Common Market agribusiness experts. They suit the City Farm Trust very well, however, and their work enables town children the informal safe access to livestock and farming practices which have become a casualty of modern methods. Included among the favourite animals are the delightful Queensway Trust donkeys who earn their keep by pulling the less-able around the valley in specially-designed carts.

The odd name of Nonsuch Farm arises from an incident in the civil war when Oliver Cromwell is reputed to have sought refuge in the barn. When cavaliers came searching for him they were told that 'none such man is here'.

Walking into Lye Close Lane it can be seen how thoughtful planning allowed the old hedges to remain despite houses being built behind, making it easy to picture the country lane it once was. Once over the stile the path lies between the conifers of the motorway embankment and the new planting of alder, willow and other trees which will one day form a belt of woodland. The fields are managed in a way which enables them to retain their abundance of wild flowers. Great burnet, field scabious, betony, sneezewort and lady's mantle mingle with the more familiar thistles, clovers and knapweeds to provide colour all spring and summer through. The hedgerows are more striking in autumn as the soft golden sunlight burnishes their changing leaves, rose hips, haws, and brilliantly-coloured guelder rose berries, whilst plump blackberries glisten with dew.

Curiously the guelder rose is not a member of the rose family, despite its name, but the plants bearing the rose hips and haws are, together with blackthorn, crab apple and cherry. This list, which is by no means complete, demonstrates how empty our hedges would be without this wonderful group of plants. Even as the beauty of the berries is being enjoyed, next year's bounty is being prepared by the hazel trees upon which the catkins of late winter are already forming.

Blackberries are perhaps the most widely picked of all wild fruit, with even 'townies' being confident of identifying this distinctive harvest. Country lore has it that any blackberries unpicked by St. Michaelmas Day – 11 October – must be left for the devil because on that day he spits on the berries and turns them sour. This demonic spite is reputed to go back to the day when Satan was thrown out of Heaven and fell into a patch of brambles. He exacts his revenge on each anniversary. A more prosaic reason could be that early October often brings the first frosts and it is these that sour the fruit.

Autumn mists and lingering dews cling to the gossamer roundels of the spider's webs, each moist droplet sparkling in the sunshine. Some of the webs are as big as dinner plates, and why not – because as far as the spiders are concerned that is what they are. Many of the larger webs are the work of the cross (garden) spider, *Araneus diadematus,* easily recognised by the white markings on its back which often form a cross. Spiders' webs are much more complex than they appear, being composed of both sticky and non-sticky threads and having a number of well-defined zones and special lines. One of these is the signal thread which can be used to locate the spider's retreat if it is not found hanging upside-down in the hub. The thread leads from the hub to the underside of a leaf or twig where the occupant sits touching it with her feet. When an insect blunders into the web its struggles cause the signal line to vibrate and the spider runs into the centre, spreads her eight legs out to locate the prey and scuttles along to grab a bite to eat. The spider's combination of artfulness and deadliness inspired this poem.

> *An unusual use for spider silk was when it was utilised as a medium for painting on for a copy of Burgman's 'Madonna and Child' which hangs in the north transept of Chester Cathedral. The original is in a church in Innsbruck.*

In the mild light of dew-hazed dawn
Arachne weaves her glimmering thread
Into an octagon of gauze,
Its deadly delicacy spread
Between the hedgerow and the gate
To trap the bright and blundering wings
Of moth and fly. Although she seems

An inoffensive artisan,
It is but cunning cleverness.
In warp and woof the quivering span
Is lengthened, strengthened, till its dire
And deadly beauty is complete,
And she may rest in modest pride,
The virtuoso of deceit.

From *The Spider*, by R. H. Grenville

Walking across old hedge lines, a flood of wild roses pours out of the hedgerow in one place, and, in another, rosebay willowherb – a plant typical of bare sites in the city – blazes brightly against the green foliage. Elsewhere the angular flower-heads of sharp-flowered rush show where this plant enjoys the slightly acid conditions found here. Nothing out of the ordinary perhaps and yet these examples are, together with many other things seen around here, an extraordinary reminder of gentler days and softer ways. Days when the Clent Hills did not have to look over the motorway, when the trees on the hill in front had not yet given their name to the Frankley Beeches service station, and when the red, white and blue sign proclaiming that establishment's existence did not intrude gaudily upon the scene.

Turn right into Kitwell Lane and then left into Balmoral Road. Turn right again by the shops and follow the path between the houses and fields until woodland is reached. Turn right into the wood over the plank bridge at the end of the iron railings.

Garden spider on its web

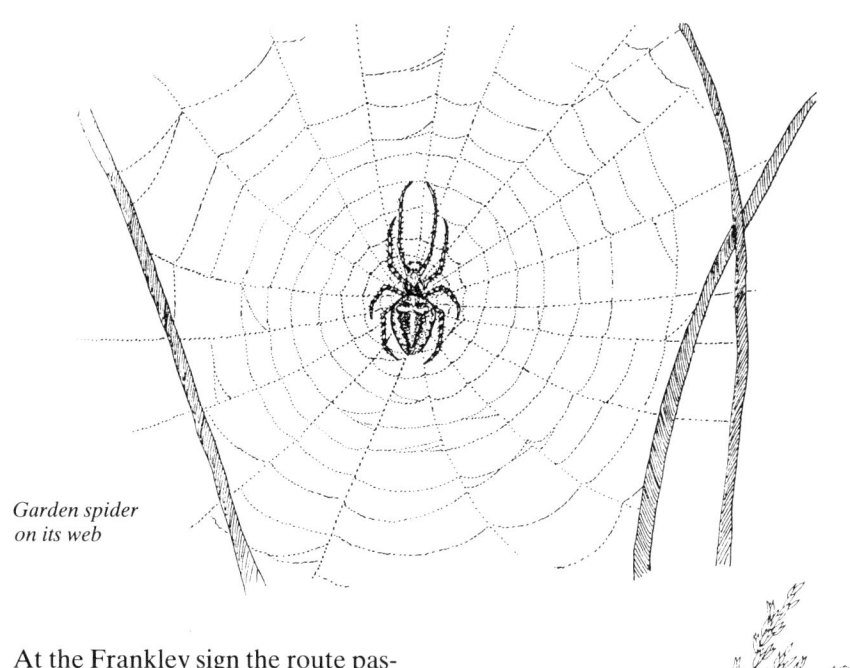

At the Frankley sign the route passes briefly into Worcestershire, the border sometimes guarded by a few geese in the field who cackle loudly when anyone walks past. On the corner of Balmoral Road there is a beautiful stand of tufted hair-grass, its tall and delicate flowerheads (panicles) shimmering in the slightest breeze, the whole bank being a pale-straw colour. This is normally a grass of damp pastures where it forms conspicuous tufts. It has leaves which feel very rough if stroked from their tips to their bases, but which feel very smooth when stroked in the opposite direction. This helps the plant to survive in grazing meadows because stock find it very uncomfortable to grasp the leaves in their mouths, and when they lift their heads the leaves slide out easily. Horses will not eat tufted hair-grass at all although cows will if there is no alternative.

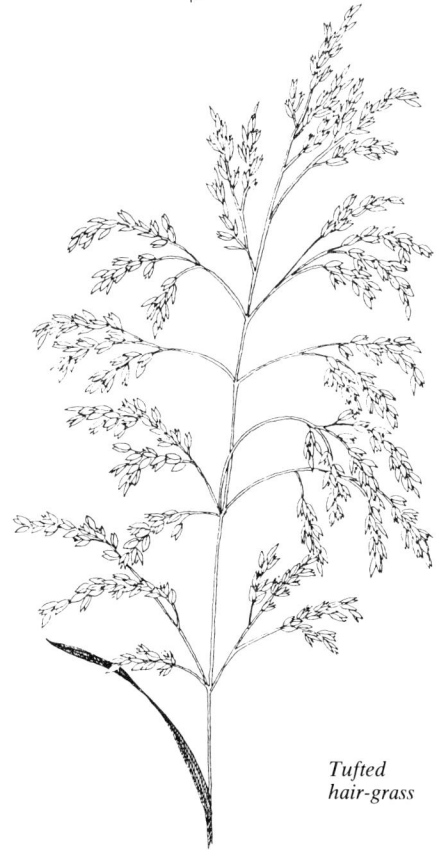

Tufted hair-grass

In the narrow passage by the shops a tiny fragment of hedgerow, consisting of hawthorn and field maple, survives as a living souvenir of the landscape which was here before the houses. It is all that now remains of a field boundary, the origins of which have been lost to antiquity, and that somehow managed to escape the fate of most of the line. The rest of path behind the houses provides a mixture of town and country, with garden birds singing on one side and black and white cows peacefully grazing in a typical patchwork setting on the other. At the end of one stretch of the path the first view of Bartley Reservoir is seen, with the dark line of the trees of Bromwich Wood to the left.

The atmosphere changes very quickly as the cool darkness of the enfolding wood is reached. Seen through the trees the water glistens and the breeze makes the shadows dance within whilst rustling the leaves high overhead. This ten acre fragment is all that remains of a once-much-larger piece of ancient woodland and it is home to a number of species which could not live anywhere else in the vicinity. In spring and early summer it is a riot of colour with bluebells, stitchwort, yellow archangel, lesser celandine and wood anemone. Moschatel is also found here – a plant sometimes called 'town-hall clock' because its greenish flowers are arranged at right angles around the top of its stem, like clockfaces on a tower. Above all of these, the oak, rowan, wild cherry, birch and alder form the canopy typical of a lowland English wood, a habitat becoming all too uncommon now.

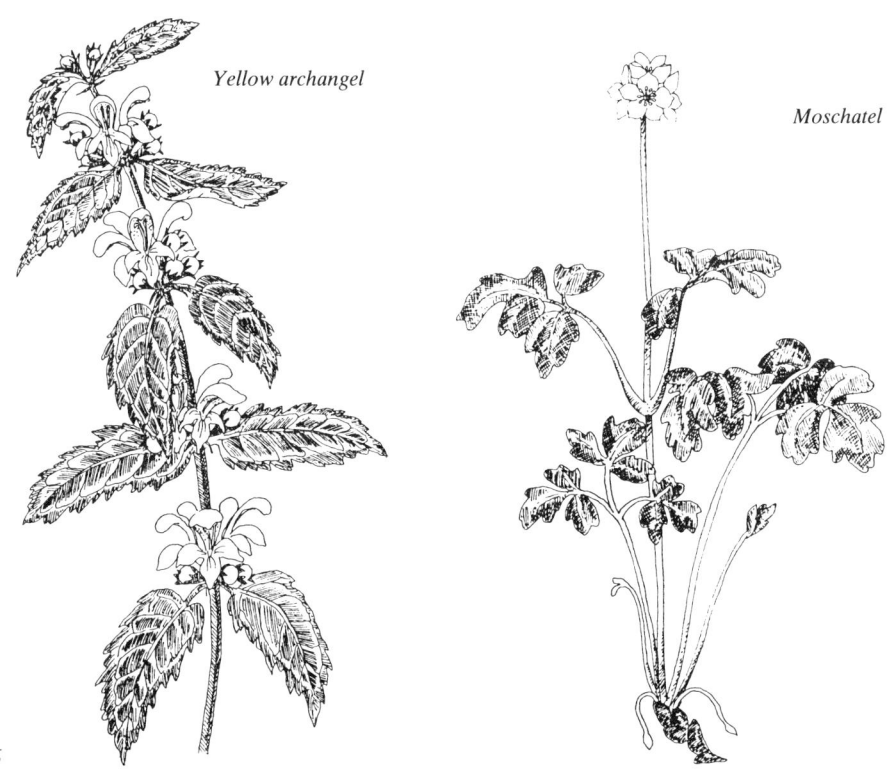

Yellow archangel

Moschatel

Make any way through the wood towards the reservoir, cross Scotland Lane and walk along the shore with the water on the right. Follow the path around the boat club and turn left into the road opposite Newman College. Cross the road and further on take the path on the right back into Woodgate Valley Country Park.

Sparkling water, liberated from the pipes which brought it from Wales but soon to be confined again to complete its journey to the taps of Birmingham, billowing dinghy sails, and a bracing breeze free from the restrictions of the wood, accompany the walker along the shore of Bartley Reservoir. Bleak and exposed in winter and with relatively bare edges, the water, even so, attracts a wide variety of waterfowl, gulls and waders. The young Bill Oddie, ex-'Goodie' and ornithologist, discovered the joys of bird-watching here. No doubt many others have been led to an interest in natural history and conservation by being able to visit such places so close to their home.

Hoverflies and butterflies search out the half-hidden ragwort flowers in the grasses to the left whilst the downy thistle heads, having earlier given up their nectar, await the winter flocks of goldfinch and linnet. These small birds may themselves fall prey to the local sparrowhawks which skim silently along the hedgerows and low over the grass, striking their victims without warning. Thus even the humble thistles have their place in the scheme of things.

The slap, slap, slap of the waves at the water's edge acts as counterpoint to the clank, clank, clank of lines on masts as the dinghies, drawn up out of the water, incessantly chatter away to each other. The boat-house marks a brief

Goldfinch on teasel

Sparrowhawk

return to buildings as Bartley Green is traversed. This Birmingham outpost, which still considers itself a village, boasts old nailer's cottages, buses called 'Wyre Forest Shuttles', and a modern petrol station proclaiming itself the 'Village Service Station'. The brilliant scarlet of the cherry tree in the street by the school is reflected in the berries and foliage of some more guelder rose planted alongside the path. A flash of white rump disappearing into a tree may be the only glimpse of one of the local bullfinches, but the magpies strut around brazenly in their piebald finery. The path goes across yet another old hedge line and over a footbridge, beneath which laughing waters gambol to a babbling confluence.

Take the left fork, pass through a small copse and turn left at Clapgate Lane. Cross over and further on turn right over a stile immediately to the left of a hedge.

Once over the stile the Woodgate Valley proper is reached again. It is the largest area of grassland in Birmingham and offers a gentle landscape of meadows, trees and hedges, lying in rural tranquility on either side of the Bournbrook. This shallow stream loiters and meanders along the valley towards a rendezvous with the River Rea near to the BBC studios. They are named Pebble Mill Studios after the original building that stood on their site and which was powered by the water of the Bournbrook. The brook is typical of many small waterways where dragonflies, water beetles and caddis flies may be found. The latter are insects closely related to moths but having hairy rather than scaly wings. Their larvae live in fresh water and many of them make protective cases from small pieces of gravel, snail shells, or vegetation, within which they live. They stick their heads and forelegs out of the case to hunt their prey but retreat inside at any sign of danger.

The traditional pedlar, who decorated his clothes with his wares, was known as the 'caddis man', and so the name was transferred to the caddis fly whose case-building mirrors that activity.

A horse chestnut and a Turkey oak (the latter is easily recognised by the long hairs at every leaf junction) stand on a small mound at the side of the path. This mound, together with others in line with it across the valley, is the remains of a spoil heap left from the building of the Lapal Canal tunnel between 1793 and 1798. At 3,795 yards in length it was one of the longest canal tunnels in the country. It took a back-breaking four to five hours to leg loaded narrowboats through the stygian dampness below. How green this valley must have seemed to the fortunate person who had the job of bringing the horse over the top whilst colleagues sweated below. In spring bright-yellow cowslips would have adorned the way and today they still grow in profusion in the area, one of the few places in this part of the Midlands where they can be found.

One end of the Lapal Tunnel is in California! It was named this by a local man, Isaac Flavel, who made his fortune in the Californian Gold Rush and on returning invested in industry around Woodgate Valley.

Cowslip

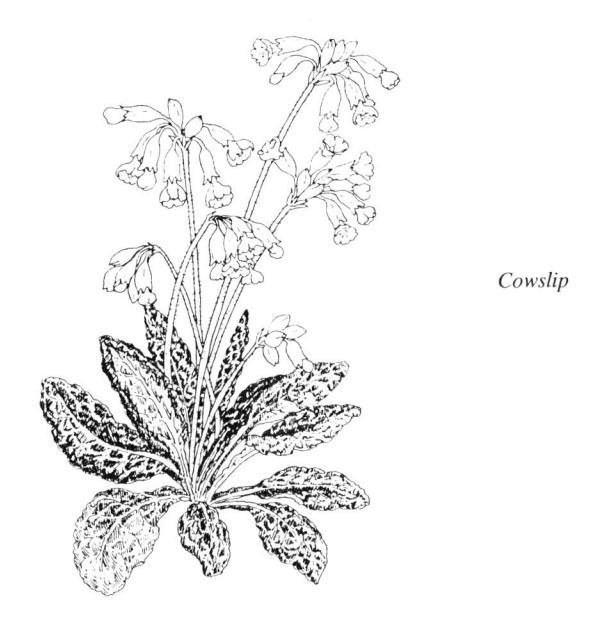

Follow the path across the meadow from the mound and cross a plank bridge. Continue until being able to turn left on to a wide path. Shortly after the willows meet over this path follow a small track to the left until a double-fenced path is reached. Turn left along this to return to the Visitor Centre.

Meadows filled with buttercups and hay rattle disguise the resident kestrel's living larder which is filled with mice, voles and shrews. This little falcon may sometimes be cheated of a meal by a terrestrial raider with whom it shares these meadows – the weasel. This lithe and sinuous creature, our smallest carnivore,

Weasel

is often seen during daylight hours sliding almost snake-like through the grass, or more probably bounding across a path with 'Lochness Monster-like' arched back. Brown above and white beneath weasels are usually solitary hunters but females out with their young may be encountered. These carnivores will take virtually any small creature that comes their way and are tiny enough to negotiate the runs and burrows of their victims. They are very inquisitive, forever foraging and exploring; even if startled to bolt into a nearby hole they can be guaranteed to poke an enquiring nose back out again quite soon. (Ireland does not have weasels, only stoats which are their cousins. Apparently combining the two, Irish stoats are called weasels!)

The little path leads into a treasure house, a patch of damp grassland packed with the priceless jewellery of the fields. In summer meadowsweet's heady scent fills the air and later in the year sheets of orange hawkweed reflect the autumn tints of the trees. Tormentil, marsh bedstraw and ragged-robin, king cups and marsh thistle – each has its turn as the seasons advance. In September and October there are hundreds of devil's-bit scabious flowers. Such rich corners have almost completely disappeared from many parts of the countryside and yet here is one in Birmingham. The Woodgate Valley could offer nothing more fitting to mark the end of a walk which, without ever getting away from the 'town', weaves a mellow countryside tapestry.

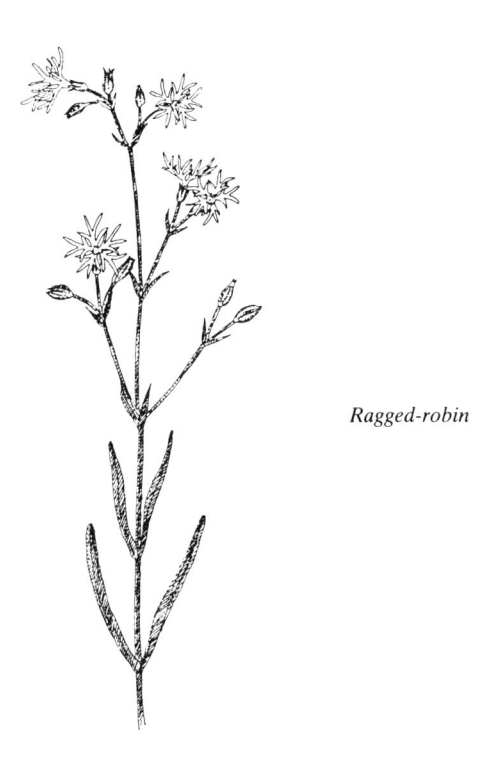

Ragged-robin

HARBORNE LINE WALKWAY

LOCATION MAP
Harborne Line Walkway

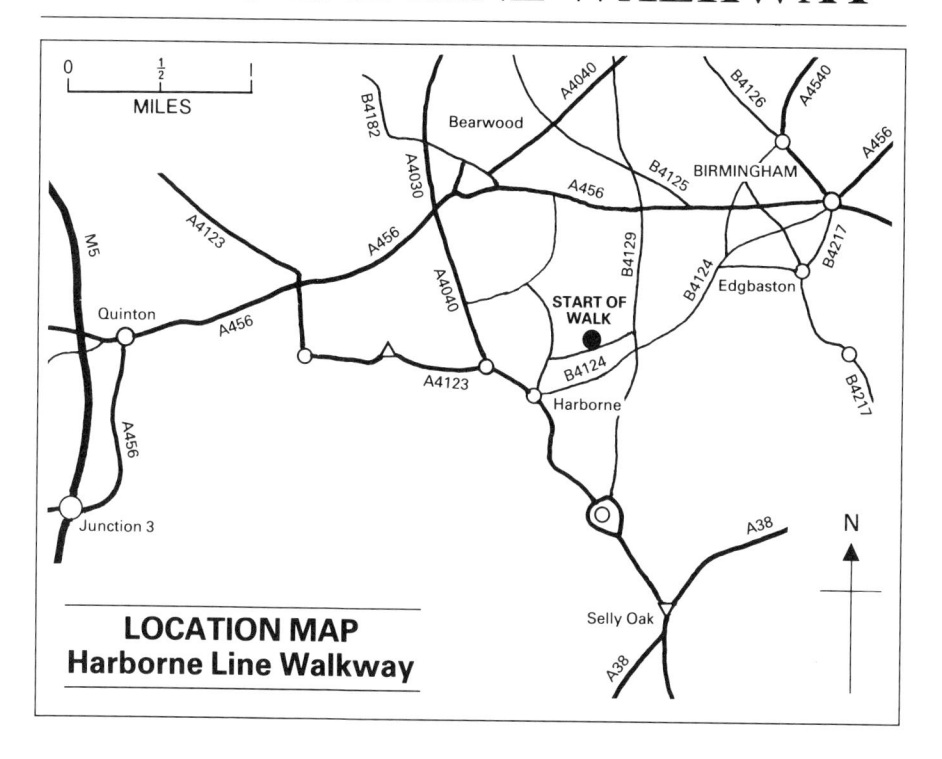

O.S. SP08 (1:25000) – 036850   Approx. 3¼ miles

An easy stroll along a well-made path with shallow steps in places. Usually dry.

Harborne Line Walkway was created along the route of a disused local railway line which closed in 1963. Its vegetation is dominated by a few aggressive species typical of rich and disturbed soil which even so includes a wide variety of other flowers, trees and shrubs. Despite being close to the city centre the walkway has a secluded woodland atmosphere. A loop from the main path takes the walker down to the Chad Brook, one of Birmingham's minor waterways. The whole route is especially noteworthy for the variety of attractive insects to be found.

The walk is so well defined that only this one set of instructions need interrupt its description. Park near to the bridge in Park Hill Road, Harborne and go through the metal 'maze' by the 'Walkway' sign. Follow the path up the ramp. After a few hundred yards look for a left fork by some horse chestnut trees and follow it down to the brook. After rejoining the main path immediately before a bridge, continue in the same direction beneath this and three other bridges to the small pool under the poplars. Turn here and retrace the route, this time staying on the top path instead of going down to the brook.

HARBORNE LINE WALKWAY

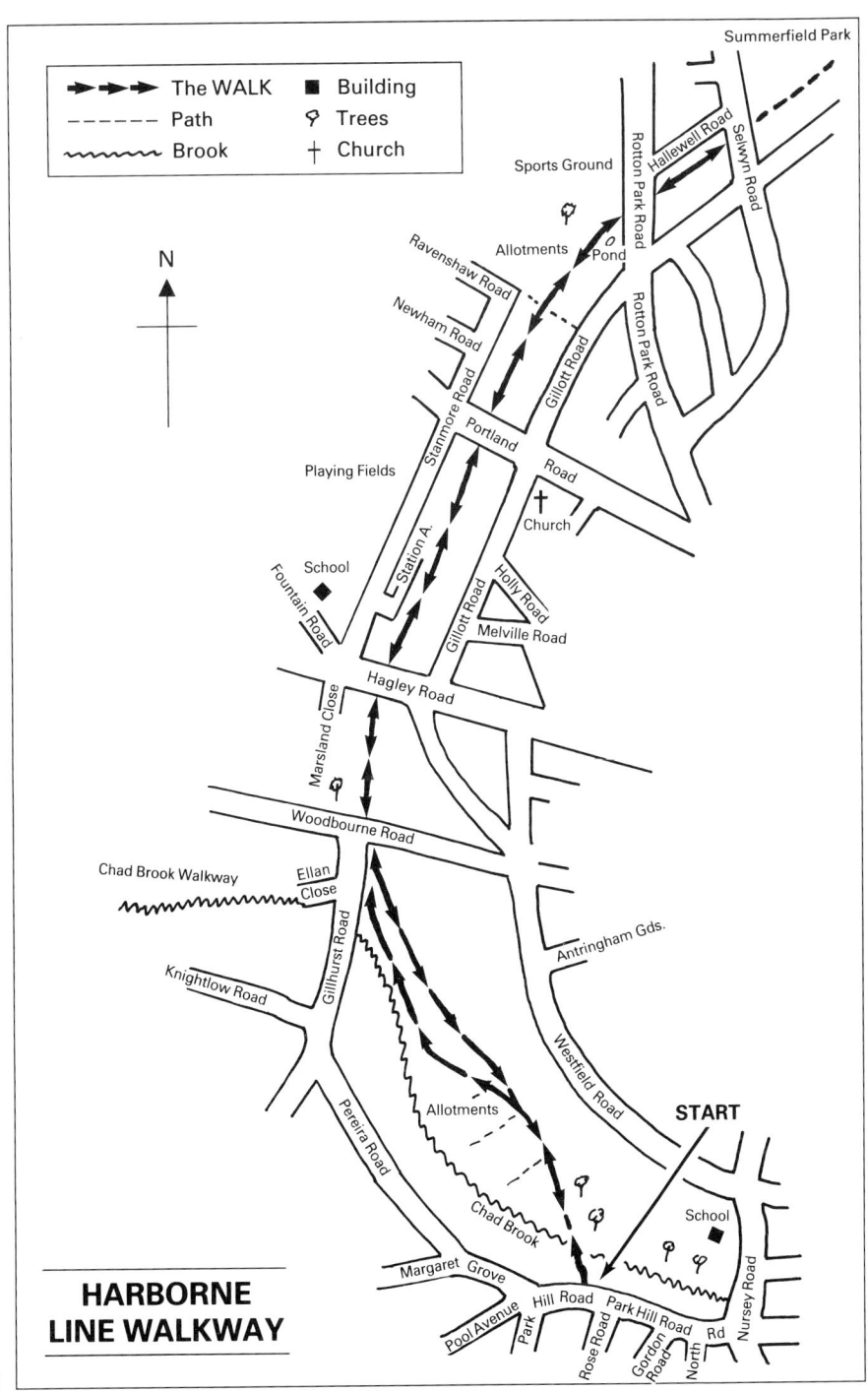

As the road is left behind, a stepped ramp stretches up and away in front, disappearing into shady greenery. Blue field scabious, red campion and herb robert beckon the walker, inviting exploration of this ribbon of nature threading its way to within 1½ miles of the heart of Birmingham. Despite passing through densely-populated suburbs and running below the main road out of the city to the west, the Walkway stays calm and quiet. Cool and shady on a hot summer's day, sheltered and protective when winter winds blow, with the world going about its business – over, alongside, and all around – it is the epitome of a byway.

The bench at the top of the ramp gives legitimacy to an early pause to take in the sights and sounds. Tall green lombardy poplars to the left lead the eye to a mauve patch where a clump of Himalayan balsam grows, a plant which will be seen in abundance further on. The gardens of the terraced houses on the right merge into more trees, and the white skeleton-like form of a silver birch is highlighted in front of the dark foliage. In the distance a multi-storey building keeps watch over the scene as magpies and wood-pigeons run aerial errands from the trees to the gardens and back again.

In late summer the brilliant-yellow flowers of Canadian golden rod can be seen in many places. This garden-escape has made itself thoroughly at home in the wild and provides a wonderful companion for the bright pink-purple rosebay willowherb with which, as here, it frequently grows. It is almost as if the gold and purple of the gorse and heather which once grew abundantly on the now destroyed heathlands around here have been reincarnated in these two plants which thrive in the urban sprawl. The golden rod provides a feast to a variety of voracious visitors from the insect world. Some of the flower-heads are covered with tiny Bibionid flies – black insects whose primitive maggots live in leaf litter and soil. Farmers consider these flies something of a mixed blessing as the adults are useful for pollinating fruit trees whilst the maggots can be a pest to hops and other crops. The insects jostling for space at the table include hoverflies – especially the bee-mimic drone fly – bees, small beetles and slender ichneumon wasps.

> *The drone fly's rat-tailed maggot lives in mud at the bottom of ponds, troughs and ditches. It survives these inhospitable conditions by breathing atmospheric air through a telescopic tube which is pushed up to the surface of the water.*

Walking past the allotments on the left the path passes from ridge to cutting. The base of the bank to the left is full of male ferns; tall and robust, they are typical of damp woods, hedgerows and shady places. Probably the most common and widespread British fern, it may be recognised by the kidney-shaped spore cases, five to seven of which will be found on the underside of each leaflet. It used to be traditional to dig up the roots of male fern on St. John's Eve (23 June), carve them into the shape of a hand and bake them, so making a charm to ward off witches and evil spirits. To do so now, of course, without the permission of the landowners, would be against the Wildlife and Countryside Act. It seems we must take our chances between magistrates and goblins!

> *It used to be believed that carrying the spores of male ferns rendered the carrier invisible despite, one assumes, all appearances to the contrary!*

Male fern

Don't forget to turn left down into Chad Valley which hosts a riot of pinks and purples as rosebay willowherb and Himalayan balsam crowd the banks on either side, enclosing the way in a soft mantle of flowers. The air hums with insects, the bees especially being attracted to the bag-like balsam blooms. Although an annual this alien species grows up to six feet high in gaudy profusion along hundreds of miles of natural and man-made watercourses, suppressing all other herbaceous plants. Its large flowers are borne on reddish stalks and consist of a broad lip, hood, and hollow spur, the inside of which is beautifully coloured with different shades of orange. The plant is variously known as Himalayan balsam and Indian balsam (both these names referring to its natural home), touch-me-not (from its seed pod's habit of exploding when touched), and policeman's helmet (from the shape of the flowers). The exploding seed capsule is the key to its spread along waterways – the ability to shoot seeds just a few feet takes many of them into the adjacent water where they float away. Some eventually become lodged in a bank, or are left high and dry by falling water-levels and so start a new colony. Unwelcome as it may be Himalayan balsam is here to stay, along with its orange-flowered relative from North America, christened 'jewel-weed'. At least our bees like it and here by Chad Brook it makes the ideal bee-study station. Honey bees, bumble-bees and solitary bees all come to imbibe its nectar and collect pollen. They rest briefly on the lip before plunging head-first into the flower, giving ample opportunity for the observer to decide whether they are white, buff, or red-tailed bumble-bees – or another type of bee altogether. The insects then reverse out dusted with pollen and lumber unsteadily into the air for the short flight to the next blossom.

Shortly, the stream appears, gurgling gleefully over its stony bed as it has for thousands of years. It is no different now from the days before Birmingham was built, before the balsam arrived, and before it had to be bridged to accommodate the invention of the wheel. Its name brought joy to thousands of Midlands children because near here stood the Chad Valley Toy Company, makers of seaside buckets and spades. How many of those buckets must have been filled with water from the brook both at home and also on the east coast, where their owners may have holidayed. Possibly many, considering that the brook flows into the Bournbrook – which the Chad meets by the BBC Pebble Mill Studios – and then the water passes on to the rivers Rea, Tame and Trent and thence to the North Sea.

Near to the brook grows comfrey, a rough hairy plant with cream or mauve bell-shaped flowers. Like others of the borage family its hairs may cause skin irritation for some people. This minor fault is far outweighed by a list of its virtues which would seem to qualify it for sainthood amongst plants. Herbalists have found many uses for comfrey and if it could cure or ameliorate half of the ills for which it is prescribed, pharmacy would be much simpler. One of its common names is 'knitbone' from the ancient use of a paste made from its ground roots in the way that plaster is used today. Besides such medicinal merits, real or imagined, its leaves can be used to make a herbal tea or may be eaten as a green vegetable. If any are left over they apparently make excellent compost.

In late summer the abundant damp and shady vegetation here and in other parts of the Walkway provide a perfect home for some spider-like creatures called harvestmen. These miniature monsters would not be out of place in a *Star Wars*-type film, most of them having eight very long legs which lift and support their one-piece body rather in the way that the roofs of some large halls are suspended from columns placed round the outside. Harvestmen scurry about like mobile hammocks eating almost any detritus that they come across. The next meal, mate or malefactor, is spied from eyes mounted on turrets (tubercles to the scientists) which add to their outlandish appearance. There are only a couple of dozen species in this country but some are very common. Unlike their close relatives – spiders – harvestmen spin no silk, possess no venom and uncaringly abandon their eggs in the manner of many insects.

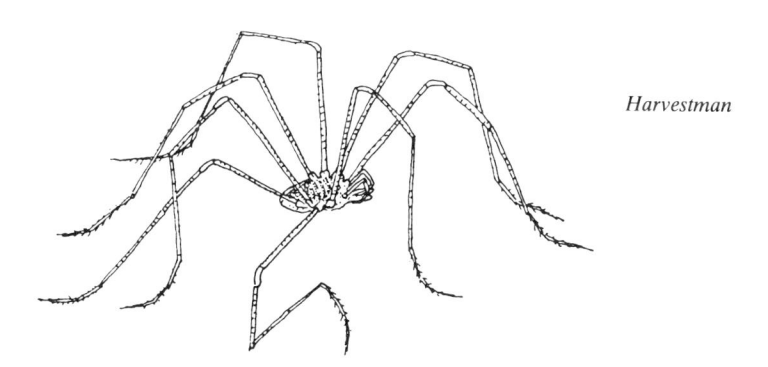

Harvestman

> House martins are multi-brooded. Parental attention to the young is extended by older brothers and sisters assisting with the feeding of later arrivals.

House martin

Climbing up from the Chad Brook the path quickly rejoins the main Walkway which goes beneath a road bridge. Mugwort with its tiny pitcher-shaped flowers, browny-red stamens and styles making each look like a miniature sea anemone. Green catkin-like nettle flowers, rushes by a tiny stream on the right, and grasses and ferns, all line the route. House martins fill the sky with a dazzling aerobatic display performed to a background of their persistent cheeps. At the clearing which marks the site of one of the railway stations, look out on the left for a plant which is, to say the least, unexpected. It is a low-growing member of the pea family, Lucerne (alfalfa), once a commonly cultivated plant in this country and still grown widely in Europe. With its violet flowers in small clusters and curious spiral seed pods which are quite distinctive it will be found scrambling over other plants by the entrance to the Walkway at the end of the cul-de-sac. What it is doing here is a bit of a mystery. Is it a relic of cultivation pre-dating the houses and the railway; was it accidentally introduced with grass seed when the area was being reclaimed, or did it arrive by courtesy of the trains running in from the countryside? Railways are after all just as effective as other transport systems for carrying unofficial cargo from the natural world. It seems quite at home now and has colonised several square yards.

Alfalfa

Just a little way further on, again on the left, two sallows alongside the path have formed an arch with dead branches. Climbing amongst these is a hop, its presence betrayed by the large-lobed and rough hairy leaves; its tough stems twine clockwise around both the sallows and each other. This plant is most likely to be a garden escape because there are no others in the vicinity. As male and female flowers are borne on separate plants it would seem to have little chance of reproducing and will therefore remain in lonely isolation.

At the end of the Walkway by the fourth and fifth bridges are some narrow pools which contain a wealth of wildlife. By one of them butterbur, with its huge flat heart-shaped leaves, grows. This somewhat untypical member of the daisy family favours damp places. It sends up the spikes which carry the lilac-pink flowers in early spring before the leaves appear. These plate-like leaves can be over three feet in diameter and contrast sharply with the narrow pointed foliage of osier, a type of willow, which also grows here. At one time it grew in extensive beds alongside the local rivers and was a valuable crop, the rights to which were sold by the lords of the manors. Its thin pliant stems (withies) were used for basket-making and thatching. The osiers here were planted as part of the rehabilitation of the old railway line.

These pools are inhabited by a beautiful dragonfly, the southern hawker, which can be seen patrolling up and down over a regular beat. It is a truly magnificent insect about three inches long with a four-inch wingspan, the male resplendent with bright green and blue markings. Often two individuals will be encountered here, each one hawking over a pool on either side of the bridge. These creatures have long given pleasure to humans as these following words written in 8th-century China demonstrate.

It is good to drink tea in the
   spring breeze,
At sunset on this flat terrace,
Inking my pen on the slanting
   stone ballustrade,
I sit down to write a poem on the
   wu-tung leaf
Here is a kingfisher singing on a
   bamboo clothes rack,
There is a dragonfly clinging to
   a fishing line,
Now that I know what quiet
   enjoyment is,
I shall come here again and
   again.

      From a poem by Tu Fu

Southern hawker (aeshna) dragonfly

Turning back down the Walkway take a look in the shallow water beneath the second bridge away from the park. In this unlikely setting lives another notable and attractive insect, the so-called water cricket, *Velia caprai*. Hundreds of these surface-dwelling and normally wingless water bugs will be discovered in the dark waters within the arch, usually clinging to the brickwork where the water laps. They are dark brown with a red stripe down each side of their bodies which are orange underneath. Here is provided a wonderful example of what may be called 'habitat substitution'. Their normal homes are upland streams or pools, peat cuttings or woodland streams. They need still or slow-moving weed-free shady water – and so what could be better than what amounts to a shallow ditch beneath a bridge? To water crickets it makes no difference what casts the shade and the brickwork allows them to indulge their habit of holding on to rough surfaces whilst waiting for their prey. They are partial to mosquito larvae of which there is no shortage here. As this area used to be heathland it is possible that this population is descended from insects which lived in pools that existed centuries ago, but as with the Lucerne it is not easy to say for sure from where they have come. It is part of the fascination of wildlife in towns and cities that the unexpected occurs alongside the predictable. The creation of 'false' habitats, the disturbance of existing populations of plants and animals, the introduction of exotic species, and pockets of relic vegetation all contribute to an exciting mosaic of natural and man-made places which create a naturalists' paradise.

Moving back down the track with dappled sunlight illuminating the dark corners, and with foxglove, St John's wort, ragwort and hawkweed showing the way, it becomes apparent that the flower of the footpath, scattered along the banks from beginning to end, is field scabious. This mauve-blue flower, a close cousin of the prickly teasel, likes well-drained grassy places and was once common in cornfields. Being a perennial it literally puts down roots where its seeds land, and so has a better chance of surviving at least limited changes in land use when compared to its erstwhile annual companions like corn cockle and cornflower. The cornfields are long gone but the scabious lingers still, a reminder of bygone days. Once cursed as a weed, then ignored by commuters and railway workers, it is now an attractive addition to suburban life.

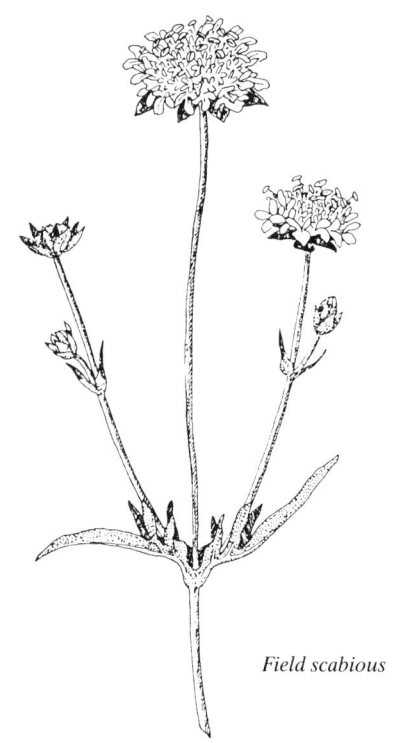

Field scabious

The benches at the site of the old station allow a few minutes' repose with the spire of St. Augustine's church providing the backdrop for watching butterflies lazily prospecting amongst the flowers. Whites, skippers, small tortoiseshells and red admirals all pass this way. In the years when conditions force them north and west, summer will bring those gilded migrants from France fluttering in – clouded and pale-clouded yellow butterflies. Almost every one seen on the Walkway will be flying north, from the Harborne end. Early arrivals will breed in southern counties, but what a nice surprise for the whitish female pale-clouded yellows passing this way to happen upon the Lucerne which is the main food plant of her caterpillars. It is rare, but not unknown, for the caterpillars to overwinter in this country, so here is a ready-made place for them almost in Birmingham city centre.

Red admiral

Moving back down into the Chad Valley area plenty of oak will be encountered. Through July and August they will be proudly wearing their mantle of new yellow-green leaves known as lammas growth. Possibly as a defence against defoliation by caterpillars, our native oaks characteristically have this spurt of new growth in mid-summer – Lammas Day is 1 August. The word is from the Anglo-Saxon, meaning 'leaf-mass' because on that day the bread used for the mass was baked from the new corn. After passing beneath the fifth bridge a reminder of this ancient ceremony may be had as the trees arch over the path from either side, darkening the way and giving the impression of walking down the nave of a natural cathedral.

The oak is often associated with paganism. As well as 'lammas bread' being utilised for mass, the first bread of the harvest was also used in a ceremony involving its burial beneath oak trees.

Just before passing back down the ramp to the street the eye is taken by a bright patch of knapweed on the right. Growing in the same place is tansy, although it often takes some recognising due to the fact that the local slugs have taken a real fancy to it. On any damp evening they will be seen all over the plants happily rasping away at the leaves with their file-like tongues. Their cousins – snails – are also much in evidence all along the route. Needing a supply of calcium to build their shells they probably thrive on a combination of the lime used by the allotment gardeners and the limestone brought in as railway ballast. No doubt the local thrushes and blackbirds appreciate this supply of mobile meat pies, a pile of broken snail shells around a rock betraying the site of an avian restaurant.

At the end of the ramp lie the houses and gardens of Harborne, and the hustle and bustle of a modern city. Yet along the Walkway is wildlife, history, peace and quiet. The spectacular and the mundane which make up the natural world is just a few steps from the shops and offices. As long as such places are kept, children will not have to ask the questions posed in this extract from a poem.

How will the legend of the age of trees
Feel, when the last tree falls in England?
When the concrete spreads and the town
    conquers
The country's heart; when contraceptive
Tarmac's laid where farm has faded,
Tramline flows where slept a hamlet,
And shop-fronts, blazing without a stop from

Dover to Wrath, have glazed us over?
Simplest tales will then bewilder
The questioning children, 'What was a
    chestnut?
Say what it means to climb a beanstalk.
Tell me, grandfather, what an elm is.
What was Autumn? They never taught us.'

From *The Future of Forestry*, by C. S. Lewis

A 'thrushes anvil' with the broken empty shells of banded snails

CHASEWATER

Chasewater and its environs provide varied habitats for a diverse assembly of animals and plants

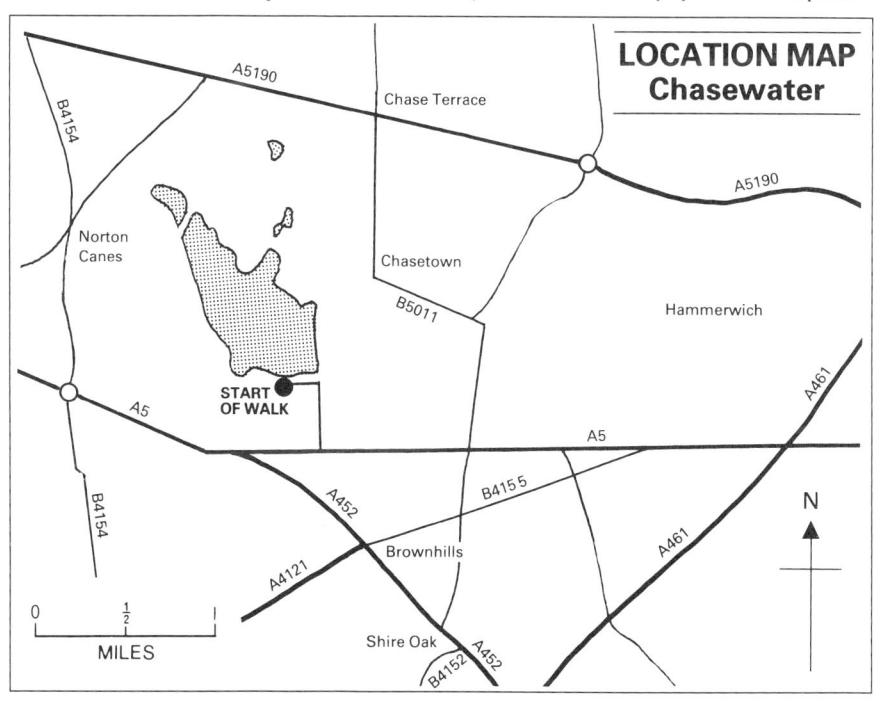

**LOCATION MAP
Chasewater**

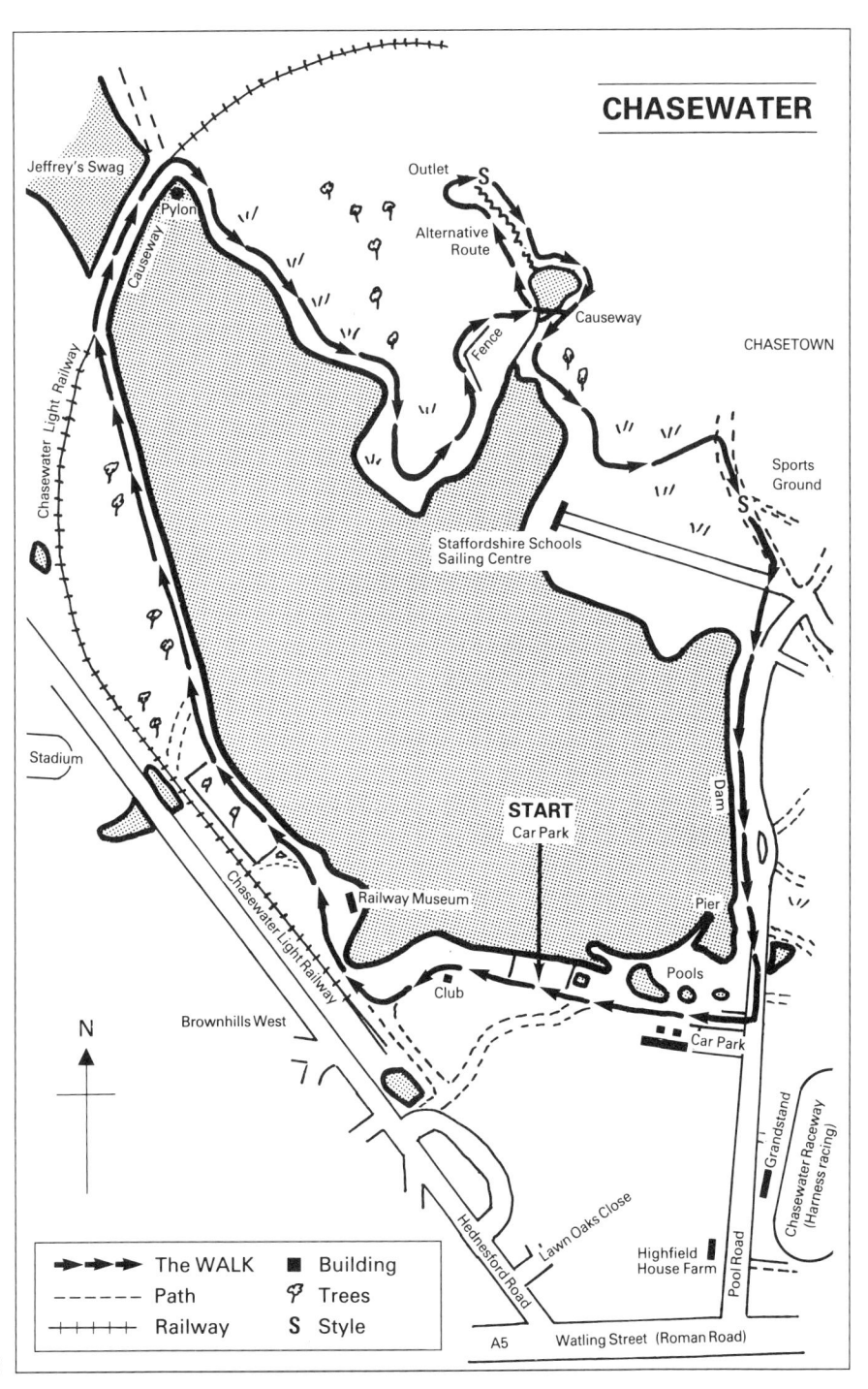

CHASEWATER

Jeffrey's Swag
Pylon
Outlet
Alternative Route
Causeway
CHASETOWN
Sports Ground
Chasewater Light Railway
Causeway
Fence
Staffordshire Schools Sailing Centre
Stadium
Dam
START Car Park
Railway Museum
Pier
Chasewater Light Railway
Club
Pools
Car Park
N
Brownhills West
Grandstand
Chasewater Raceway (Harness racing)
Pool Road
Lawn Oaks Close
Highfield House Farm
Hednesford Road
A5 Watling Street (Roman Road)

➤➤➤ The WALK	■ Building	
------ Path	𝒬 Trees	
+++++ Railway	S Style	

CHASEWATER

O.S. SK00 (1:25000) – 037071   Approx. 5 miles

A walk around the perimeter of a lake built in the Mid-19th century. Nearly all flat walking but very wet in places.

Now the second largest body of open water in the region (Blithfield Reservoir being larger), Chasewater did not exist until about 145 years ago when it was constructed to help control water levels in the Wyrley and Essington Canal. It is in the extreme north-east of the county of West Midlands, in fact the boundary with Staffordshire crosses the water. Like all lakes and pools people are attracted to it and it has become a focal point for both formal and informal recreation in the Brownhills/Norton area. Surrounded by, and containing, a very important and diverse assembly of plant and animal species distributed amongst a matrix of varying habitats, it is perhaps best known for the massive gull roost which forms each winter evening.

Park in the south shoreline car park. This is reached by turning left (signposted) off the eastbound carriageway of the A5 near Brownhills and, after passing the trotting track grandstand, turning left through the gates into Chasewater. Pass the car parks on the left and proceed to the shoreline car park on the right.

Commence walking with the lake to the right, pass the railway museum rolling stock and around the powerboat club. Step over the low rail by the padlocked gates.

It is evening in late March. Seven swans in stately synchrony slide along the water's edge. The pristine white feathers and bright-orange bills of two adults contrast with the brown and white plumage and pale bills of the juvenile birds. A pied wagtail, tiring of its examination of the grit at the edge of the car park, gives one last shake of the tail before flying away. Skimming over the swans, the wagtail's undulating flight gives the impression that it is 'buzzing' each of the larger birds in turn. A pair of mallard suddenly appear, to descend rapidly to the middle of the water and are lost below the horizon, a distant cloud of spray marks their feet-first landing.

Pied wagtail

93

This introduction to Chasewater highlights one of its main natural history attractions – the birds. Birdwatchers come from far and near to see, for example, terns, cormorants, Iceland and glaucous gulls, and goldeneye ducks. Over 200 species have been recorded in recent years. Not that Chasewater, or Norton Pool as it is also known, is a particularly secluded or even peaceful retreat for its feathered guests. Carved into the heathland forming the southern flank of Cannock Chase in order to serve the canal system of Victorian industry, its origins were prosaic. Now surrounded by housing, mining and manufacturing, its present circumstances are not obviously propitious for wildlife, but seen beneath a wild sky filled with wheeling, calling birds it is evocative of the wilderness that once held sway all around. Because of the use people make of the water, Chasewater is of more value to birds for resting, roosting and feeding than for breeding. Its size and location are the keys to its attraction and virtually any species can turn up during autumn and spring migrations. In March 1987 the first little scaup (an American duck related to our tufted duck) to be recorded in Europe made an appearance here.

> Although cormorants are seabirds and nest on rocky coasts, they also live inland. Breeding colonies are found on large bodies of water and nest nearby in trees. They can be tamed and used to catch fish for their owners.

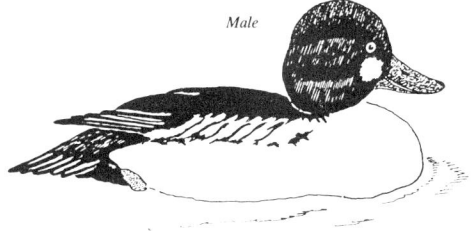

Female

Male

Goldeneye ducks

In spring the air around this part of the lake is filled with skylarks rising to accompany the walker with mellifluous melody, bringing to mind the appropriateness of the collective noun 'exultation' for a company of these exuberant songsters. The poet Shelley was inspired by such a one now watches to make sure careless feet do not crush next year's choristers.

Hail to thee, blithe spirit!
Bird thou never wert –
That from heaven or near it
Pourest thy full heart
In profuse strains of unpremeditated
*   art.*

Higher still and higher
From the earth thou springest,
Like a cloud of fire;
The blue deep thou wingest,
And singing still dost soar, and
*   soaring ever singest.*

In the golden lightning
Of the sunken sun,
O'er which clouds are bright'ning,
Thou dost float and run,
Like an unbodied joy whose race is just
*   begun.*

The pale purple even
Melts around thy flight;
Like a star of heaven,
In the broad daylight
Thou art unseen, but yet I hear thy
*   shrill delight.*

From *Ode to a Skylark,* a poem by P. B. Shelley

Follow the old railway line to the right over the causeway between the two pools.

Crossing the causeway listen to the pot-pourri of sounds converging. The hum of traffic and perhaps the barking of a dog from the nearby houses make a strange contrast to the crows, cawing as they would in a mountain valley, and the raucous raft of gulls in the middle of the water, evoking thoughts of a seagirt stack far from this part of the West Midlands. The water to the left is called Jeffrey's Swag and is the most popular bird-watching spot at Chasewater. For the less-able-bodied the opposite shore offers the facility of being able to watch and study a surprisingly diverse range of water birds from a car. In winter up to 100 goldeneye and 500 tufted ducks will be found here.

On either side of the causeway, great crested grebes will usually be seen diving in the scrub-invaded shallows for fish. If swans are the monarchs of the water then these beautiful birds must be the courtiers, resplendent with chestnut cheeks, dark crests, dignified deportment, and elaborate courtship routines. Perhaps ambassadors for their kind would be a more apt title as it was the threat to their continued existence from the plumage trade which brought the Royal Society for the Protection of Birds into being. The down from the breasts of these grebes was used as an alternative to fur which proved so popular that they nearly became extinct. Their salvation has resulted in the conservation of many other species as well. Always wary and watchful (they have not yet learned to recognise an RSPB badge!) they never venture too near the shore.

Summer plumage

Great crested grebes

Winter plumage

This area can also provide sightings of an unusual bird for this part of the country and one which is easily overlooked as it falls into the class of birds non-ornithologists call 'little brown jobs.' It is the twite, a finch closely related to linnets, redpolls and siskins. Both sexes have yellow bills in winter but they do not have any red on the head or breast. The twite is the northern and upland counterpart of the linnet and as such is at the edge of its range at Chasewater.

Turn right by the pylon which has all its feet in the water and follow the shore as best you can. Paths in this area are not well defined and the water line varies. Keep going until a post and wire fence is reached then follow it to the left away from the water. Turn right where the fence turns right and walk towards the inlet in front of the sailing school.

The heathland here is one of the two most important and diverse areas of botanical interest adjoining the lake, being close to the site of Norton Bog which is frequently mentioned in 19th-century literature. The other area is the Anglesey Basin to the north of the dam. Whilst casting about for the way, it will soon become apparent that the vegetation is in fairly well-defined zones. Along the shore is a band of willow carr, many of the trees standing in open water; next is an area dominated by rushes, a group typical of infertile soils; then there is a swathe of brilliant-green star-shaped mosses, a species of *Polytrichum* which form a deep, springy carpet; finally, the mosses merge into and then give way to heather where the land becomes drier.

All around here plants typical of the heathy parts of Cannock Chase, some of them Staffordshire specialities, will be encountered. Particularly noteworthy are the 'berries' – bilberry, cowberry, cranberry and crowberry, as well as the rare hybrid between the first two. This is known either as the 'hybrid bilberry' which may qualify it for a prize for the plant with the most boring name, or the 'Cannock Chase berry' which is marginally better. All except crowberry are members of the heath family and bear edible fruits. Crowberry is the single representative of the family *Empetraceae* in this country. They are all low-growing shrubs generally found on acid soils of heath, moor and bog. The hybrid bilberry was first discovered in Britain on Camp Hills in Staffordshire in 1870. Specimens were sent to no less a luminary than Charles Darwin who was reported to have expressed pleasure that the discovery was made in an area to which he was so much attached. In 1898 it was found close to the southern shore of Chasewater in Norton Bog. Bilberry, which has a characteristic black berry with a purple or violet bloom, was well known to the old herbalists. Culpepper says of it 'It is a pity they are used no more in physic than they are.' They have been used to treat fevers, agues and coughs.

Bilberry

Bilberries or whortleberries as they are called sometimes were a saleable crop at country fairs. In the last century they were sold at Stafford market for 3d a pint. Wolseley Park was famous for its bilberries in the 17th century.

The insect life of Chasewater is very apparent in this area. Water-breeding insects like gnats and midges perform their aerial ballets and, believe it or not, they are not all waiting to pounce on unsuspecting humans. The orange-tip butterfly may come in search of a member of the cabbage family upon which it lays its eggs. Here, the all-white female will favour the cuckoo flower (lady's smock), whilst the partly-orange male takes the eye as it flits over the vegetation. Britain's commonest butterfly, the small heath, will be seen (its caterpillars feed on grasses), as well as the small copper whose food plants are docks and sorrels.

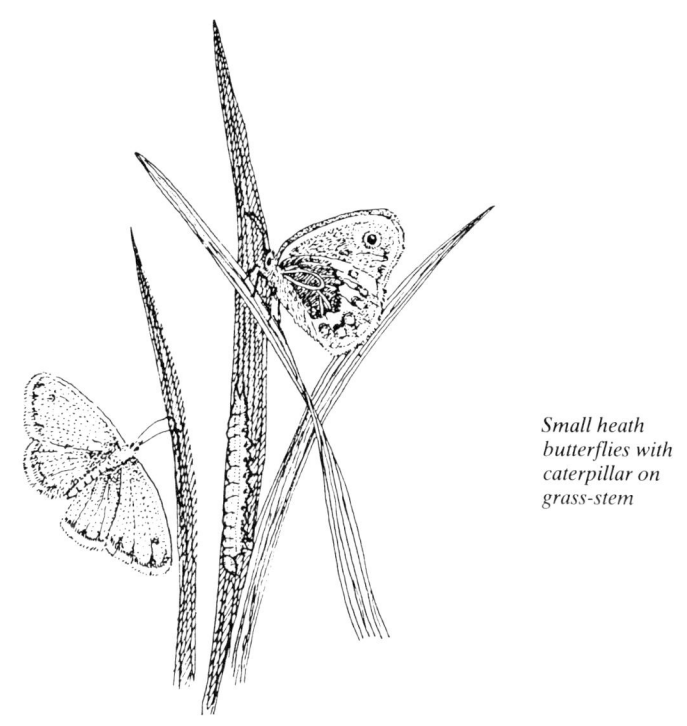

Small heath butterflies with caterpillar on grass-stem

As the route moves away from the water over slightly drier ground the larks again become prominent. The heather begins to mix with gorse and broom – both members of the pea family. They are able to thrive in relatively poor ground because of their ability, shared with the rest of the legumes, to fix nitrogen in the soil for their own use. The white nodules found on the roots are a type of gall produced by bacteria associated with the plants and which are the vectors of the fixing process. Whatever time of year it may be, gorse flowers will be seen as they bloom in all seasons. This phenomenon endeared the plant to country folk and gave rise to the saying, 'Love's in fashion when gorse is in bloom.'

The plant broom was the emblem of Geoffrey Count of Anjou, father of Henry II. One of its old scientific names was Planta genista, *hence 'Plantagenet' of English history.*

When the water is reached again turn left. If the level is low enough cross towards the sailing school over the red-ash causeway, climbing the steps up the opposite bank.

If this is not possible continue to the stream and, using the telegraph poles as a guide, bear left then right to find the crossing point by the last pole. The way here is ill-defined. Cross the stile and walk back down the opposite bank. Follow the red-shale path around the back of the school. Climb over the stile by the sports pitch and go down the main track to the right of the double poles. Where the path joins the road either go straight on or, if the sun is setting, turn right and walk to the shore by the sailing school.

On any damp evening in spring or summer care must be taken to avoid treading on the numerous black *Arion* slugs which emerge in the hour or so before dusk. These shell-less molluscs need a constantly damp environment hence their crespucular (twilight) or nocturnal appearances. During daytime and 'drytime' they retreat beneath logs and stones and lurk in dark crevices. They eat a wide range of vegetable matter and the following 'instructions to collectors' of these animals were no doubt born of constant frustration: 'The nature of locality records, etc., made at the time of collection will vary with the nature of the investigation, but remember that *slugs eat paper and cardboard:* labels should be on the *outside* of any container.'*

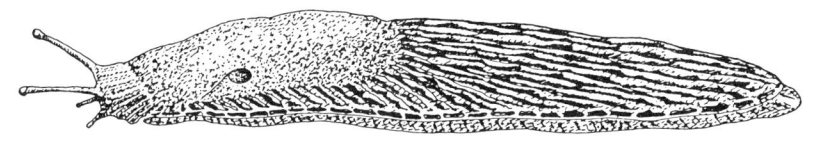

Arion slug

With the right amount of cloud cover sunsets at Chasewater are breathtaking. Reds, oranges, greys, pinks and blues above and below the horizon dazzle the eye. The most spectacular time of all to experience the view is midwinter. It is then that Chasewater's special attraction will be seen. Anyone who moves around the West Midlands' conurbation during a winter afternoon will notice two sorts of bird on the move in considerable numbers. Flocks of starlings will be assembling and flying towards Birmingham city centre; they fly from perch to perch in noisy parties which grow in size as they meet and merge. High above them small groups of gulls, usually between three and 20 in number will be flying north-east. Chasewater is their destination and by the time darkness falls as many as 15,000 will have arrived to roost for the night. When all of the ducks and other waterfowl are added this is probably the largest single concentration of water birds between the Midlands and the west coast estuaries of the Dee and the Severn. Their calls carry far across the water and when they are disturbed the whole roost rises in great commotion, hangs in mid-air for a few moments looking like a snowstorm, then drops down to a slightly different place. It all happens as if the flock is a single entity rather than thousands of

*Quotation from *A Field Guide to the Slugs of the British Isles* by Cameron, Jackson and Eversham Field Studies Council, Publication S14, 1983

Great black-backed gull

individuals. To see this against a fiery sunset is to be transported in spirit away from the surrounding houses to those wild places that perhaps only exist in our imaginations nowadays. The whole atmosphere is primeval and stands comparison with almost any other offering of the natural world in this country. The majority of birds in the flock are either black-headed, lesser black-backed or herring gulls, but there are also likely to be scores of great black-backed gulls, as well as the much rarer kittiwakes, Iceland and glaucous gulls.

The goldeneye ducks mentioned earlier will also be witnessing the spectacle. They are another of Chasewater's specialities and their numbers have been increasing in recent years, spending winter here before migrating to Scandinavia and Russia to breed. They do not really seem to know whether to be birds of water or air: they nest in places such as old woodpecker holes in pine trees, but dive more deeply for their food than many other species of duck, frequently going to depths of 20 feet or more. Their favoured food is either snails or crustaceans. Goldeneyes are quite distinctive having triangular-shaped heads that are glossy green-black on the drakes and chocolate brown on the ducks. The drakes have a prominent white spot between the base of the bill and the eye. Both sexes have white necks, broad white wing bars and yellow eyes.

Keeping the lake to the right make for the end of the dam to walk along the path between the dam wall on the right and a narrow tarmac road on the left.

On the opposite side of the road to the dam is an extensive area encompassing a mixture of habitats including remnants of the original dry heathland, damp grassland, acid bog and marshland. A very rich flora has developed along with stands of heather, bracken and reedmace. Tormentil, a yellow cinquefoil having only four petals instead of the five its relatives have, grows not far away from its showier cousin, marsh cinquefoil. The latter has the right number of petals – five – contained in star-shaped reddish-purple flowers. It reverses the normal pattern of flowers, however, as the petals are narrow and pointed and quite insignificant in comparison to the broader, more spreading, sepals.

Round-leaved sundew

Marsh cinquefoil

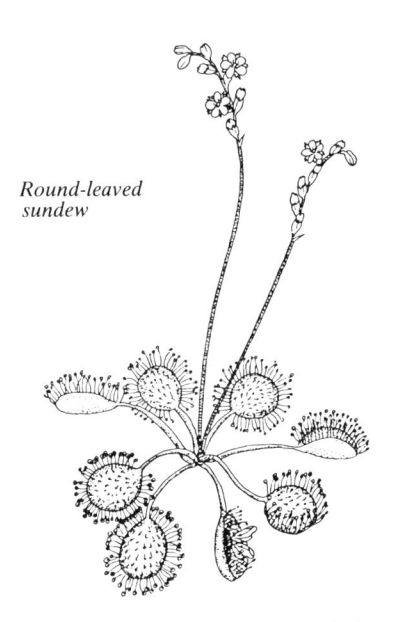

Both tormentil and marsh cinquefoil are intolerant of lime and they are joined in this area by a plant which has evolved in a very special way to survive in the improverished environment of acid bogs. This is the round-leaved sundew which traps insects on sticky hairs on its leaves, enfolds and then digests them to supplement an otherwise meagre diet. This is a rare example of the flora getting its own back on the fauna for all the browsing and grazing it does, or as an unknown poet put it:

What's this I hear
About the new carnivora?
Can little plants eat bugs and ants
And gnats and flies?
A sort of retrograding!

Surely the fare of flowers is air,
Or sunshine sweet.
They shouldn't eat
Or do aught so degrading.

A poem from *Wild Flowers Month by Month in Their Natural Haunts*, by Edward Step, Frederick Warne, 1905

Charles Darwin published his work *Insectivorous Plants* in about 1875, thus bringing this odd group of plants to general attention. At that time sundews were common and well distributed, in fact some farmers wrongly thought that they caused liver disease in sheep grazing on boggy land and accordingly called the plant 'red-rot.' The real culprit was, of course, the liver fluke which passed part of its complicated life-cycle as a parasite on mammals and part as a parasite on snails. Today sundews are much less common, being victims of the drainage boards and agricultural improvers. In Staffordshire they are found in only eight or nine places.

Charles Darwin had many connections with Staffordshire. His grandfather, Eramus, lived in Lichfield, near Chasewater, and became associated with the Wedgwoods. Charles was a grandson of the famous Josiah Wedgwood and married his cousin, Emma Wedgwood.

At the gates turn right and return to the car park.

GALTON VALLEY

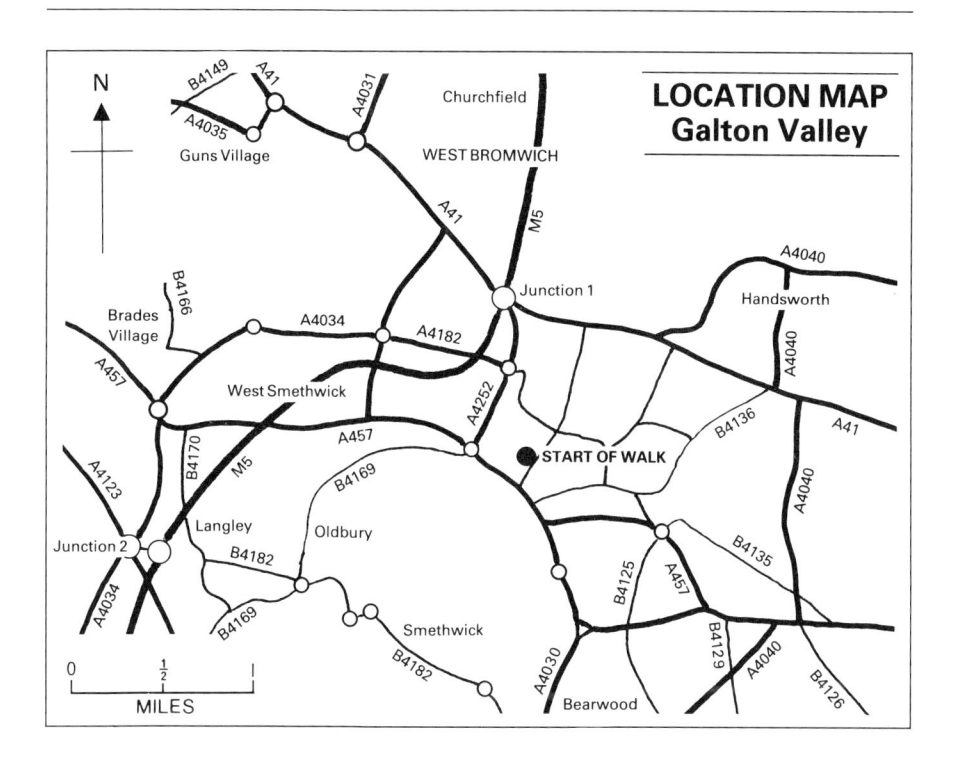

O.S. SP08 (1:25000) – 019890   Approx. 1½ miles

A walk along canal towpaths in the Galton Valley – a man-made cutting – in the heart of the industrial Midlands. Natural and industrial history share this renowned site which was a vital transport artery during the Industrial Revolution. There is a steep bank and some steps to negotiate; the towpath can be muddy.

Despite being within yards of Smethwick High Street and a main railway line this is a surprisingly peaceful and green oasis. It has not one but two canals, their banks changing colour with the seasons as the grasses, flowers, shrubs, and trees bloom and fade; and birds, animals and fish find a living here. The clamour and smoke of the 19th century and the massive upheavals of the 18th century are but a memory. Many of the bridges and locks around the valley are listed buildings or scheduled ancient monuments. The jewel in the crown is the ornate Galton Bridge, spanning the deepest part of the cutting made to accommodate Telford's New Main Line in 1829.

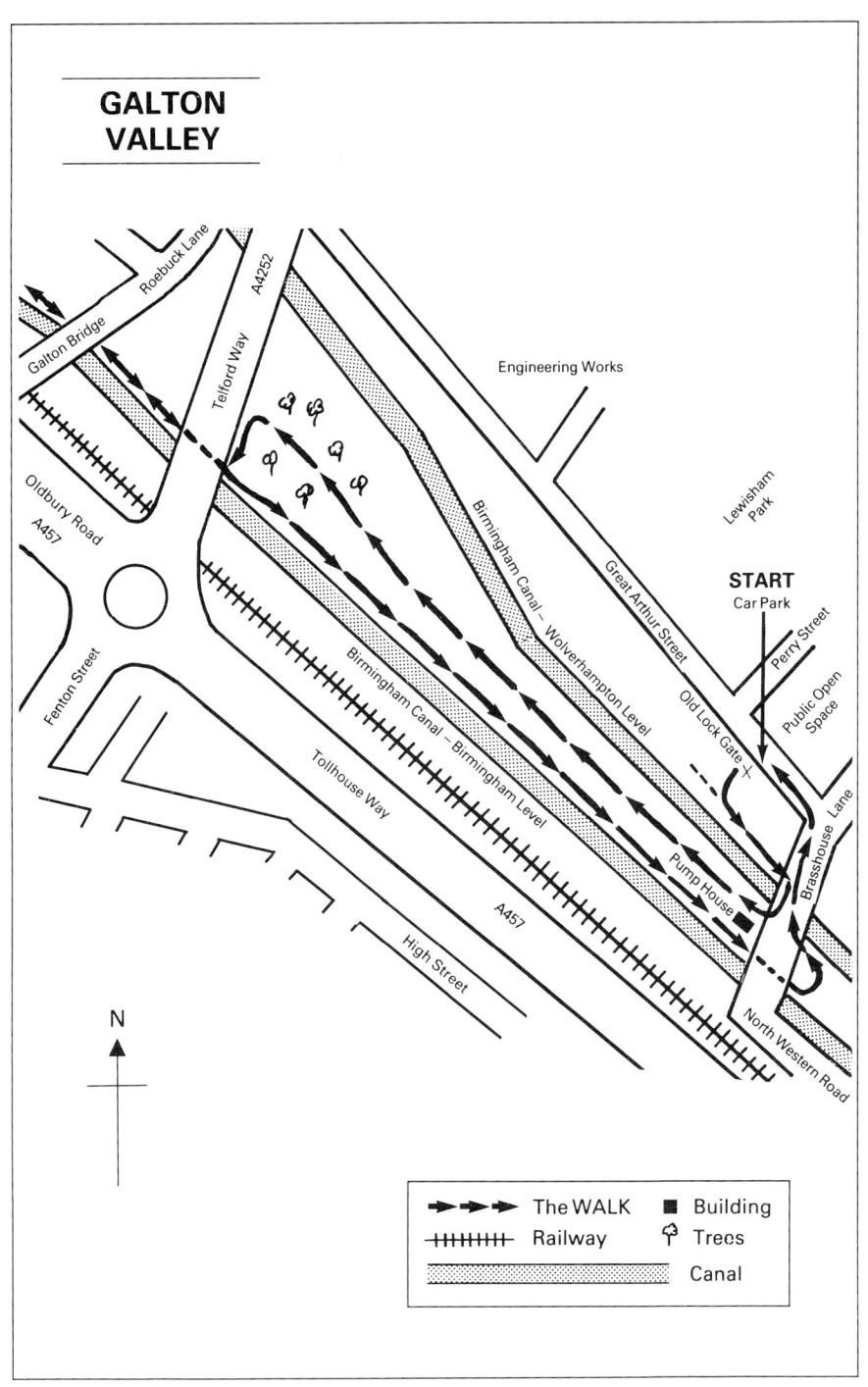

GALTON VALLEY

Engineering Works

Roebuck Lane
Galton Bridge
A4252
Telford Way
Oldbury Road
A457
Fenton Street
Birmingham Canal – Wolverhampton Level
Birmingham Canal – Birmingham Level
Tollhouse Way
A457
High Street
Great Arthur Street
Lewisham Park
START Car Park
Old Lock Gate
Perry Street
Public Open Space
Pump House
Brasshouse Lane
North Western Road

N

➤➤➤ The WALK
┼┼┼┼┼┼ Railway
▓▓▓ Canal
■ Building
♣ Trees

102

Park in the car park in Great Arthur Street. Turn left just past the old lock gate and go down the steps. Turn left at the path junction, right at the road, and cross the first canal. Turn right down the steps and proceed along the towpath.

Between the car park and the road bridge is a newly seeded and planted area typical of many such places in towns and cities. Sites like this have a habit of producing all sorts of wild flowers which were not on the nurseryman's list. They will change from month to month and year to year as the conditions become more stable, short-lived annuals giving way to more permanent biennials and perennials. The three types are normally represented here in late summer by field pansy, weld, and yarrow respectively. The shifting population of itinerant annuals may consist of any number of different plants such as groundsel, scentless mayweed, shepherd's purse, black nightshade, or poppy. Some of these opportunists, or weeds as others may call them, 'find' such temporarily attractive sites by means of parachute-like structures attached to their seeds which allowed air currents to waft them away. Those which land on poor bare soil will find little competition from other species and will germinate, flower, set seed, and launch a new generation of seeds in less than a season. Ultimately more permanent settlers arrive, stake their claim to the available light and nutrients and force the botanical gipsies either to the margins of the plot or to seek their fortune wherever the next temporary, or ruderal, site may be.

Field pansy

Some seeds will not germinate if the light falling upon them is infra-red. This is because leaves are transparent to infra-red light and it would indicate that the place where they are is overshadowed by other plants.

At the top of the steps the nation's transport history is laid out across the valley: Smethwick High Street, a dual carriageway, a main railway line, and two canals will be seen. The canals lie in a deep cutting, the sides of which are covered in a variety of grasses, wild flowers, shrubs, and trees. They are now the possessors of land that has seen the line of the old toll road expanded to take in the main road from Oldbury to Birmingham, the Wolverhampton to Birmingham railway line and three canals. These were built across and then through the 'Smethwick Summit' by, each in turn, Smeaton, Brindley and Telford. Across the High Street to the left of here stands a restored toll house, a reminder of the days when through-travellers were expected to pay for the extra upkeep needed to ensure that the main roads were kept in some sort of repair. Did Robert Louis Stevenson perhaps pass through here when thinking of writing this now-famous poem?

Faster than fairies, faster than witches,
Bridges and houses, hedges and ditches;
And charging along like troops in a battle,
All through the meadows the horses and cattle:
All of the sights of the hill and the plain
Fly as thick as driving rain;
And ever again, in the wink of an eye,
Painted stations whistle by.

Here is a child who clambers and scrambles,
All by himself and gathering brambles;
Here is a tramp who stands and gazes;
And here is the green for stringing the daisies!
Here is a cart run away in the road
Lumping along with man and load;
And here is a mill, and there is a river:
Each a glimpse and gone for ever!

From *From A Railway Carriage*, by Robert Louis Stevenson

The cutting of not one but three canals was undertaken here because of congestion at the locks; queues of impatient boatmen sometimes literally fighting for the next lift or drop. The successive lowering of the level enabled flatter straighter routes to be used thus cutting out both time-consuming meanders and some of the locks. This exactly mirrors our current problems with roads – as they fill up, wider, straighter, flatter ones are constructed. Perhaps we should ponder on the fate of the canals which became commercially redundant within a few decades of their hey-day.

> *England's first canal, Car Dyke, was built by the Romans between the rivers Nene and Withan. In 1566 another was built connecting Exeter to the Exe Estuary. The modern system was commenced in 1761 by the appropriately named Duke of Bridgwater.*

Each transport system has left its mark upon what used to be an area of heathland. So much so that almost all trace – but not quite all – of the original habitat has disappeared. It is still possible, for example, to find plants like heather and broome growing on the sides of the cutting, the remnants of the vegetation which once flourished undisturbed for centuries on this part of the Birmingham Plateau.

Leaving the bustling High Street and busy railway line behind and above and dropping down to the canal towpath takes the walker into another world within minutes. In place of the town sounds, the gentle splash of a water vole or frog dropping into the water and making for the opposite bank, or the chattering of a flock of sparrows and finches foraging amongst seedheads, may be heard. The chirruping of grasshoppers announces their presence in the unmown sward. Late on a summer's evening, when the setting sun bathes the pink-purple flowers of rosebay willowherb in golden light, the area takes on the appearance of a remote hillside covered in heather – a curious irony when it is remembered that there is now very little heather left here and the rosebay willowherb is a relative newcomer.

Grasshopper

The reed sweet-grass which fringes the opposite bank provides a perfect dwelling place for moorhens. Their waterside nests are relatively safe alongside the canal as the water level does not go up and down as much, or as quickly, as that of a river. In addition the roots and stems of the grasses act as a sort of shock-absorber against the wash of slow-moving narrowboats. Moorhens are colourful members of the water-rail family with red and yellow bills, green legs, dark bodies and white under-tails. They are very common on rivers, ponds, and marshes throughout Europe and parts of Africa, Asia and America. Unusually it is the female of this species which will fight for a mate and her aggressive behaviour does not stop there. Moorhens are included in a small group of birds which may be evolving into parasites as cuckoos have already done. Their extra-marital egg-laying is restricted to another moorhen's nest rather than those of other species of birds, and it has been well-recorded that they will search out neighbours upon whom to inflict their offspring. It is presumably not beyond the bounds of possibility that two birds will swim past one another after each has laid in the other's nest! Males and females incubate the eggs – wherever they may have come from – and, as two or three broods a year are common, young birds from earlier broods will often assist with the raising of later arrivals. As well as being partial parasites they are also partial migrants, northern populations moving south for the winter whilst southern populations stay put. They are certainly not the world's best fliers, suffering from a very laboured take-off – definitely jumbo-jet rather than Harrier – after which they do not seem capable of retracting their undercarriage, so that their legs dangle in an ungainly fashion. Despite these aerial shortcomings some of them nest in trees rather than at water-level, and inflict upon themselves the extra burden of having to carry their chicks in their feet when they are ready to be introduced to the water. Once in the water, moorhens have a characteristic jerky swimming action and are capable of diving beneath the surface. They eat both plant and animal matter but are mainly vegetarians. Variously known as water hens, moat-hens, moor-coots, and mere-hens (from which their most recent name is derived) they were once regarded as excellent eating themselves.

Moorhens

Go to the left of the brick wall and follow the path uphill for some way to the road.

Here is the derelict garden of Galton House. This glorious tangle of vegetation provides a home for countless insects which buzz, crawl and jump around this mini-jungle. Forget all you have heard about nasty creepy-crawlies and try to see what is going on amongst the tall grass stems. Maybe armour-plated ladybird beetles will be lumbering along looking out for the greenfly upon which they feed. If they are out of luck perhaps something else has got there first, such as an assassin bug with its fearsome needle-like mouthparts which it plunges into the aphid's body to extract the fluids. Other predators include long-bodied dragonflies and narrow-waisted wasps with shimmering wings which pierce the aphid with their ovipositor, in order to lay their eggs inside.

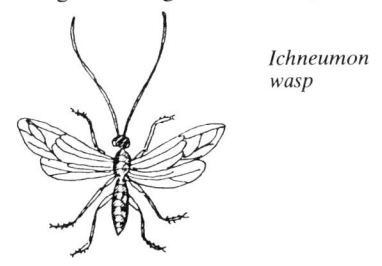

Ichneumon wasp

The great thing about places such as canal banks and derelict gardens is that because nobody comes along to mow or tidy them every couple of weeks, hundreds of plants and animals are able to thrive. Existence may still be a struggle, but at least it is possible! Lurking in the long grasses of July and August those insect musicians, the grasshoppers, saw away like cellists, their so-called chirping being a noise made by rubbing their legs against their wings. It can be quite an experience to sit quietly for a few minutes to listen to this sound, properly called stridulation, and to try to work out where and how many of these insects there are. The long grass favoured by the grasshoppers is also used by the beautiful dark-grey and pink day-flying burnet moths. These creatures use the stems as supports for their papery cocoons, which can be found, sometimes in large numbers, high on the stalks of cock's-foot or timothy grass. The stems are not, as is sometimes thought, used as food: the caterpillars in fact feed on clovers and vetches, whilst the adult moths, which fly in July and August, take their nectar from flowers such as teasel and thistle. This use of various species of plants at different times in an animal's life-cycle illustrates the importance of diversity in the urban landscape to a great number of creatures. If they are to survive and produce future generations to delight our senses we must help to provide more than just green spaces.

Near the straggly remains of an old hawthorn hedge the scarlet berries of bittersweet scramble through the branches of other plants. The berries are the final metamorphosis from purple and yellow flowers through green and then yellow berries – a plant which rides around the rainbow picking out the colours as it goes. The light-brown stems of a miniature forest of raspberry canes stand out against the bright green of those of the broome, a plant which has such tiny leaves that its stems help in converting the sun's light into energy through photosynthesis. This miraculous process is achieved through the medium of chlorophyll which in turn is what makes plants green, hence the brilliant-green stems of the broome.

Although the water is different to that which the poet Lord de Tabley had in mind, this poem could have been written for this part of the Galton Valley in winter.

1. *Grass afield wears silver thatch;*
   Palings all are edged with rime:
   Frost-flowers pattern round the latch;
   Cloud nor breeze dissolve the clime;

2. *When the waves are solid floor,*
   And the clods are iron-bound,
   And the boughs are crystall'd hoar,
   And the red leaf nailed aground.

3. *When the fieldfare's flight is slow,*
   And a rosy vapour rim,
   Now the sun is small and low,
   Belts along the region dim.

4. *When the ice-crack flies and flaws,*
   Shore to shore, with thunder shock,
   Deeper then the evening daws,
   Clearer than the village clock.

5. *When the rusty blackbird strips*
   Bunch by bunch, the coral thorn;
   And the pale day-crescent dips,
   New to heaven, a slender horn.

From *A Frosty Day*, by Lord de Tabley

At the top of the hill is a small plateau and a grove of trees which includes horse chestnut, oak, beech and Turkey oak. The latter is an exotic oak, being a native of Southern Europe and South-West Asia which was introduced to this country in the first half of the 18th century. It is now common in parks and large gardens and is easily distinguished from other oaks by the hair-like growths at each bud and the soft moss-like covering of the acorn cups.

Turkey oak showing foliage and acorns

Often found growing around here is a beautiful little cup-lichen – a type of *Cladonia*. Looking like so many miniature green wine glasses the cups bear spore-producing bodies around their rims. As with all lichens *Cladonia* are an intimate association of an algae and a fungus. The resulting spores are only able to reproduce the fungus and so for the lichen to propagate itself it must encounter cells of the algal partner. There are many different sorts of *Cladonia* and another which is common in this area has red-tipped stems instead of cups and is known as 'devil's matchsticks'. In the cold latitudes of the Arctic Circle a further example – reindeer moss – is often the most abundant plant and it sustains huge herds of reindeer and their North American counterparts, caribou.

Just before the road turn left inside the fence and drop down to the towpath. Turn right through the tunnel and walk as far as the second bridge over the canal. Turn here and walk back along the towpath to the Pump House.

This egg-shaped tunnel is the newest on the canal, having been created in 1974. Unlike conventional tunnels it was not driven through an inconvenient hillside to make a way for the canal, rather it was placed in position and the hill then put on top to carry a new road. It is ironic to think of all the effort taken with pick, shovel and barrow to dig out the cutting only to have this part filled in again. Walking through it, provides a wonderful surprise view of one of the most beautiful pieces of canal hardware in the country – Galton Bridge. The next bridge along, a solid brick structure, is clearly visible before the nearer but higher and lighter Galton Bridge suddenly appears, soaring over 70 feet above the water. Built in 1829 to take the now redundant road over Telford's New Main Line, its 150-foot span arches elegantly overhead. It was the state-of-the-art when it was built – a designer bridge bringing art to artefact. It was once the world's longest single-span metal bridge, crossing the world's largest man-made earthwork.

The results of all that shovelling and burrowing are clear to see in the deep cutting through which the canal now passes. In effect the hill which formed Smethwick Summit has been turned inside-out. The original slopes around this part of the Birmingham Plateau have been built on, but they have been replaced by these artificial inclines which allow wildlife to flourish in the very heart of the industrial landscape. Some of the plants have descended from the former inhabitants, some are newcomers, but they blend together gently to mould, colour and clothe this green valley which runs down to the limpid water. Someone once described this part of the country as an endless village. If this is so then the canals must be the endless village pond.

> *It is still possible to travel by water from apparently land-locked Birmingham to the Irish Sea, the North Sea, the Thames Estuary, and the Bristol Channel along the canal system.*

One animal which finds canalside life to its liking is the fox. One of the few carnivores left in this country, together with members of the badger, weasel, and stoat family, plus the rare Scottish wild-cat, it has adapted well to urban life. Welcomed and even encouraged by many townspeople, rarely persecuted and never hunted, with food of all sorts in abundance and plenty of garden sheds to make an earth beneath, life is pretty easy for a lot of these red raiders. Foxes' adaptability has held them in good stead whilst other creatures have come and gone.

Resident here since before the days of the mammoth, foxes have survived more recent co-inhabitants such as the bear, wolf and wild boar, and show no signs of being under any pressure at all. It makes many a person's day to catch a glimpse of a sleek russet fox, with its button-bright eyes, white-tipped brush and pointed ears, reading the morning breeze with upturned muzzle, before setting off with the determined trot that distinguishes it from the domestic dog which lurches and meanders along.

Fox

On the bank to the left, bracken, foxgloves, knapweed and tansy may be seen. Tansy was much used by herbalists in the treatment of sciatica, toothache, gout and worms. It grows to about three feet and has fern-like leaves and is one of those members of the daisy family whose flowers only have disc florets (like the middle of a common daisy flower). To the right of the path, in the cracks of Telford's stone-coping at the water's edge, will be found a plant with bright-green leaves which look like miniature Christmas trees. It has whorls of pale, purple-spotted flowers at the base of the leaves. This is gipsywort, a plant typical of the water's edge and which finds canal sides very amenable. Its name derives from the dark dye made from a tincture of its foliage. Ne'er-do-wells would have used this to darken their faces when about their nefarious activities and if there were any gipsies in the area it would have made it easier to blame them for the misdemeanours.

Tansy

Examination of the gipsywort may well lead to a flurry of activity beneath the water as the looming shadow of the examiner sends shoals of three-spined sticklebacks diving for the safety of deeper water. Found in abundance in these waters the males become another sort of 'red raider' during the breeding season, the undersides of their bodies turning red at this period. Unlike the moorhens the male sticklebacks do all the fighting and the nest-building, and are doting parents. They make a nest of plant bits and pieces in which the female is persuaded to lay her eggs. Guard is then mounted over the eggs and, later, the young fry, ensuring that they do not stray too far too soon. If this does happen the fry are gathered in the mouth of the adult stickleback and transported back to the nest. The name of stickleback comes from the three spines along their back which are raised when combating intruders on their territory. Generally speaking they are about two inches long and are found in every sort of water, including the sea. They feed entirely on water animals such as daphnia or cyclops. Sticklebacks remain almost every small boy's introduction to fish, being an ideal size to inhabit the average jam jar for the hour or so before interest wanes and some new activity is embarked upon.

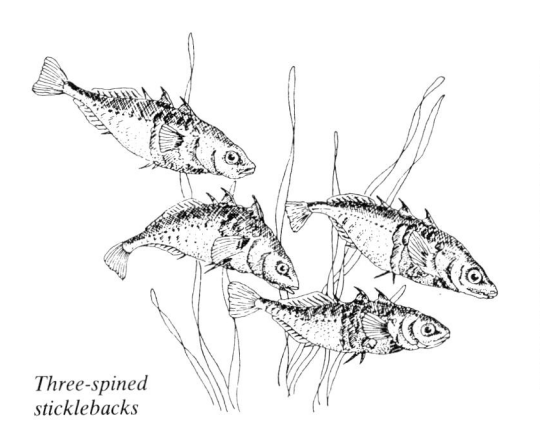

Three-spined sticklebacks

The famous naturalist Tinbergen discovered that male sticklebacks adopted threatening postures whenever the postman parked his red van outside the window near to where he kept some in a tank. This led him to discover much about their territorial behaviour.

Just past the Pump House, go under the bridge and turn immediately left and left again up a brick ramp. Cross the road and return to the car park.

The Pump House is relatively new compared to many of the other canal buildings in the area, having been opened in 1892 to house two steam-engines. These lifted water from the New Main Line to the Old Main Line to replenish losses from the higher canal at the nearby locks. Its restoration is part of the recreational development of the canal cutting which is now named the Galton Valley Canal Park. Sandwell Metropolitan Borough is responsible for this imaginative scheme, first started by the now defunct West Midlands County Council. Such ventures are needed if a happy medium is to be found between over-tidiness and sterility on the one hand, and neglect, fly-tipping, and the domination of an area by rank growth on the other.

In October and November the waters mirror the autumn tints of the trees along the banks, white gulls wheel and mew, and hawthorns stand adorned with rich red fruit ready to feed the blackbirds and thrushes. These birds are happy for now to find their tit-bits in the leaf-litter. Trains, boats and cars speed through the narrow valley, but Mother Nature still finds space to care for her own.

KEYS TO IDENTIFYING WILDLIFE

Unfortunately space does not permit the inclusion of a key to all the species that may be seen on these wildlife walkabouts. Instead, the following notes have been set out on the particular features to look for if a species is encountered that is not recognised. These notes should help the walker to jot down the important clues which will be a guide to correct identification when reference books at home or public library are consulted. It is even better if field guides are taken on walks – a flower guide is especially useful as it will help to resist any temptation to take a specimen away, which, apart from destroying the pleasure of others, is very likely to be against the law. A notebook and pencil are invaluable on any walk.

The following pages contain notes on:

Birds – general identification points
– beak types
– feet types

Plants – general identification points

Ferns – general points
– illustrations

Trees – general identification points
– illustration of bud, leaf, flower, fruit, seed and general shape of a horse chestnut tree

Mammals – general identification points
– fur on wire
– hazelnut clues
– skulls and bones
– animal tracks

Insects and Spiders – general rules of classification
– illustrations

BIRDS

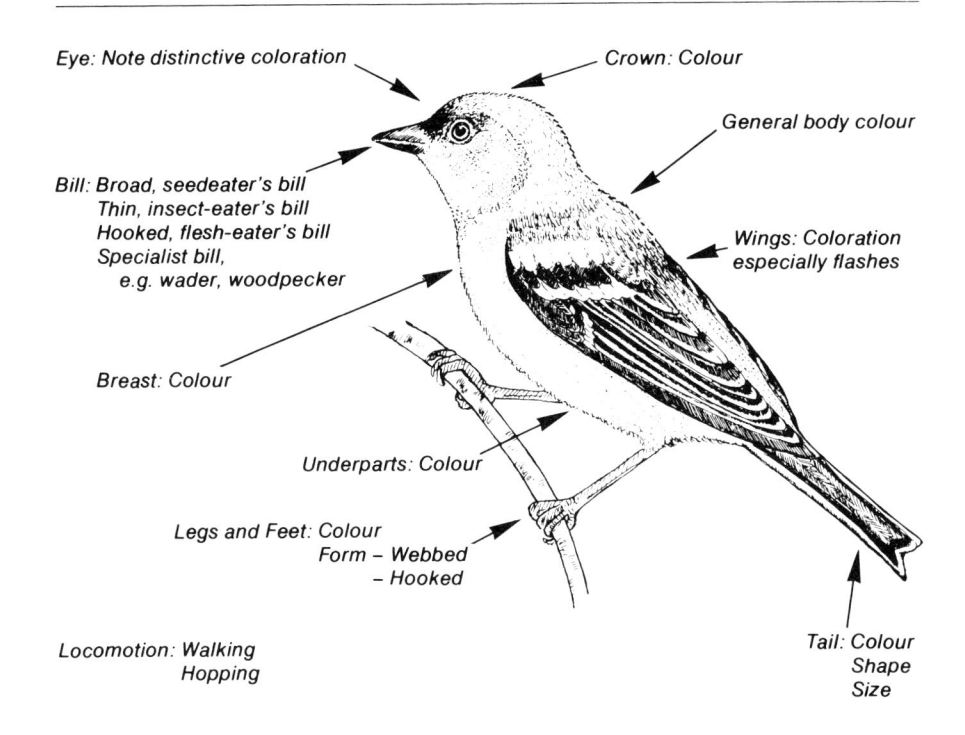

Eye: Note distinctive coloration

Crown: Colour

General body colour

Bill: Broad, seedeater's bill
Thin, insect-eater's bill
Hooked, flesh-eater's bill
Specialist bill,
e.g. wader, woodpecker

Wings: Coloration especially flashes

Breast: Colour

Underparts: Colour

Legs and Feet: Colour
Form – Webbed
– Hooked

Locomotion: Walking
Hopping

Tail: Colour
Shape
Size

Size: in relation to say a blackbird or starling.
Habitat: where seen, e.g. arable land, coniferous woodland.
Activities: feeding on the ground, clinging to tree-trunk, etc.
Time of year.
Area of country.
Sounds: turn them into words if possible, e.g. cer-loo (curlew call).
Behaviour: e.g. feeding continuously; short run, feed, short run.
Flight: flight pattern – dipping, hovering, soaring, etc.
  speed
  altitude
  purposeful or localised – hunting insects, fish, displaying, etc.
  shape of wings – rounded, pointed, swept back, etc.
Water birds:
  swimming and diving for some time
  swimming and bobbing under
  swimming and upturning with head under and tail in air
  diving from branch or air.

BIRDS' BEAKS

Broadly speaking, small birds can be divided into two types by their bills. Those with fine slim beaks are insect-eaters while seedeaters have broader more powerful bills. There are, however, a large number of specialist feeders that have evolved beaks of a shape suited to their diet. Flesh-eaters have hooked beaks for tearing their prey, waders have long beaks for probing sand and mud, and ducks have flat bills for sieving their food from the water.

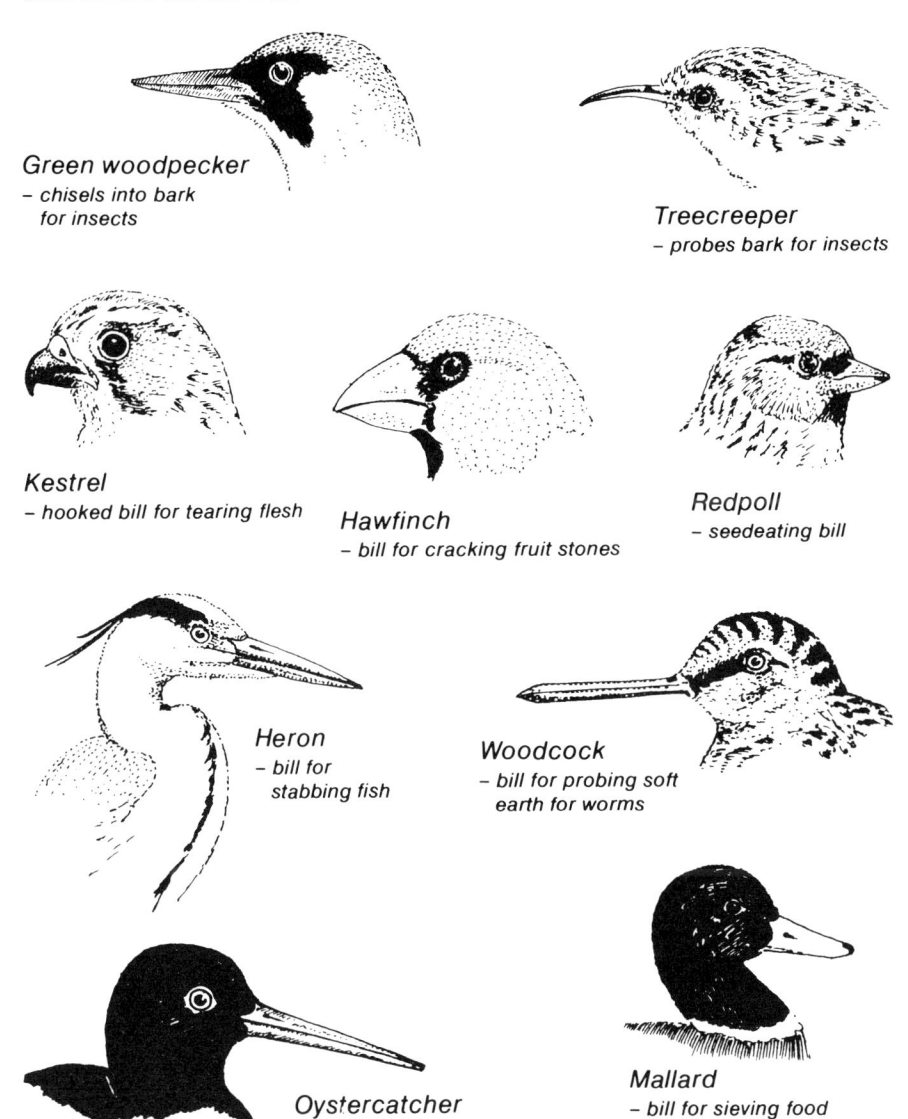

Green woodpecker
– chisels into bark for insects

Treecreeper
– probes bark for insects

Kestrel
– hooked bill for tearing flesh

Hawfinch
– bill for cracking fruit stones

Redpoll
– seedeating bill

Heron
– bill for stabbing fish

Woodcock
– bill for probing soft earth for worms

Oystercatcher
– bill for prising open shells

Mallard
– bill for sieving food from water

113

BIRDS' FEET

The more specialist birds have evolved feet to suit their habits and environment, e.g. the webbed feet of water birds which enable them to swim quickly. This specialisation tends to make water birds much slower on land, and the more aquatic their lifestyle, the less mobile they are out of water and in extreme cases, such as divers, they can hardly walk. At the other end of the scale are coots and moorhens – equally adapted to moving on land and in water. Their feet have lobes on the toes to increase their width when swimming and yet enable them to run unhindered.

Other birds with specialist feet include the predators which have sharp claws for seizing their prey. Woodpeckers have two toes facing forwards and two backwards which allows them to cling to vertical tree trunks with their feet holding the bark in a clamp-like grip.

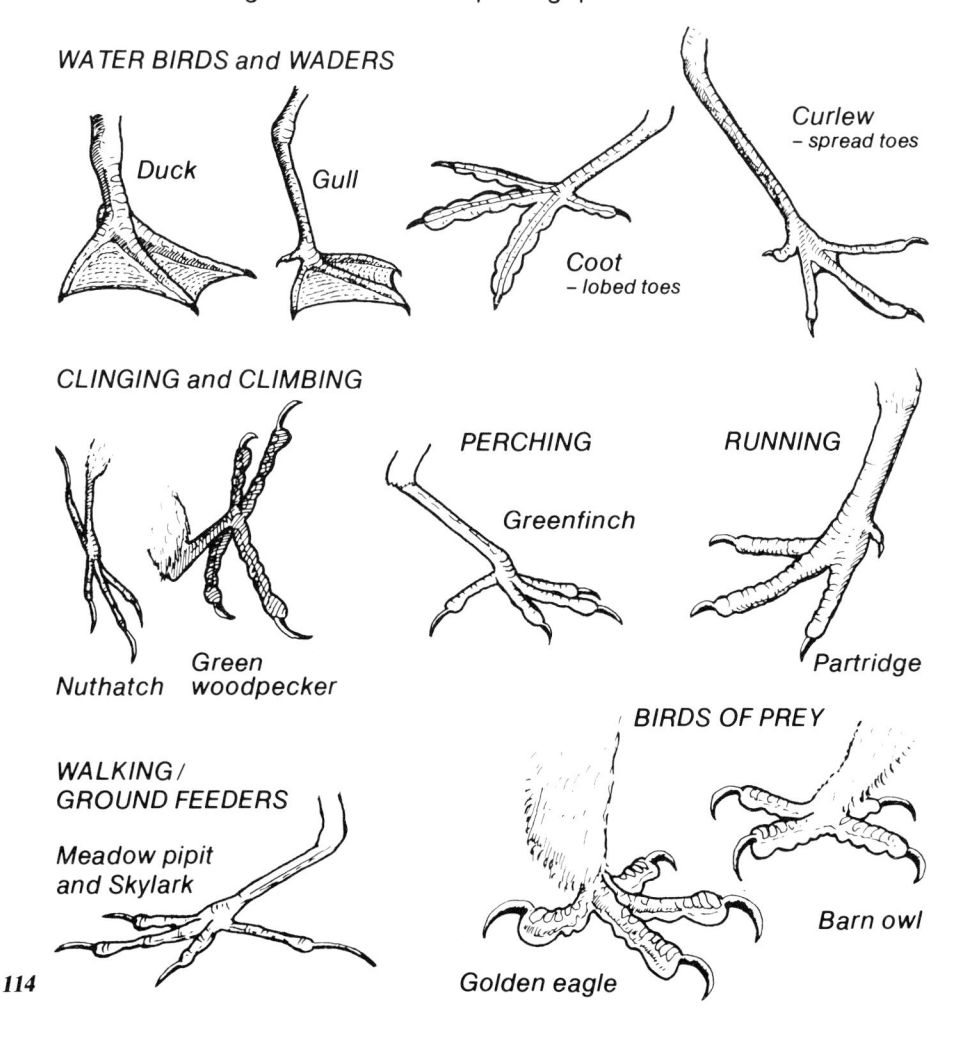

WATER BIRDS and WADERS

Duck

Gull

Coot
– lobed toes

Curlew
– spread toes

CLINGING and CLIMBING

Nuthatch

Green woodpecker

PERCHING

Greenfinch

RUNNING

Partridge

WALKING / GROUND FEEDERS

Meadow pipit and Skylark

BIRDS OF PREY

Golden eagle

Barn owl

PLANTS

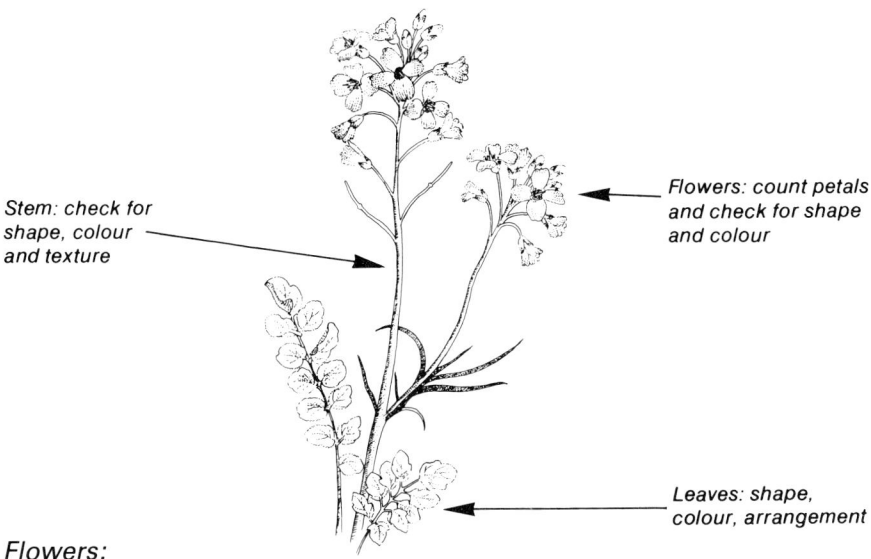

Stem: check for shape, colour and texture

Flowers: count petals and check for shape and colour

Leaves: shape, colour, arrangement

Flowers:
colour
general shape, e.g. 'traditional flower'
composite flower like the dandelion
asymmetrical like the foxglove
number of petals, petal shape – rounded, pointed, toothed, etc.
arrangement – single flower on stalk, clustered, several clusters, etc.
size of flower
scent.

Stem:
cross-sectional shape: gauge by feel
texture: smooth, hairy, prickly, etc.
height
colour.

Leaves
arrangement on stem
edges toothed, saw edged, smooth, convoluted, etc.
veins – prominent, different colour, etc.
peculiar coloration
texture – hairy, dull, shiny, etc.

Seeds: colour, size, how dispersed.

Environment: chalk, limestone area, moorland, etc.

Habitat: hedgerow bottom, stream bank, limestone pavement, peat bog, hazel wood, etc.

Time of year.

FERNS

Ferns are primitive flowerless green plants the ancestors of which formed present-day coal deposits. On the undersides of fern fronds are brown circular discs which are groups of spore sacs. Either wind or animals disperse the tiny spores, which are released when the sacs split, and from each spore grows a small green disc containing both the male and female parts of the plant. It needs a film of rainwater to enable the sperms to travel to the female egg sacs for fertilisation to occur, and this requirement for a moist climate means the ferns are more common in the humid west of Britain. The illustrations are not to scale.

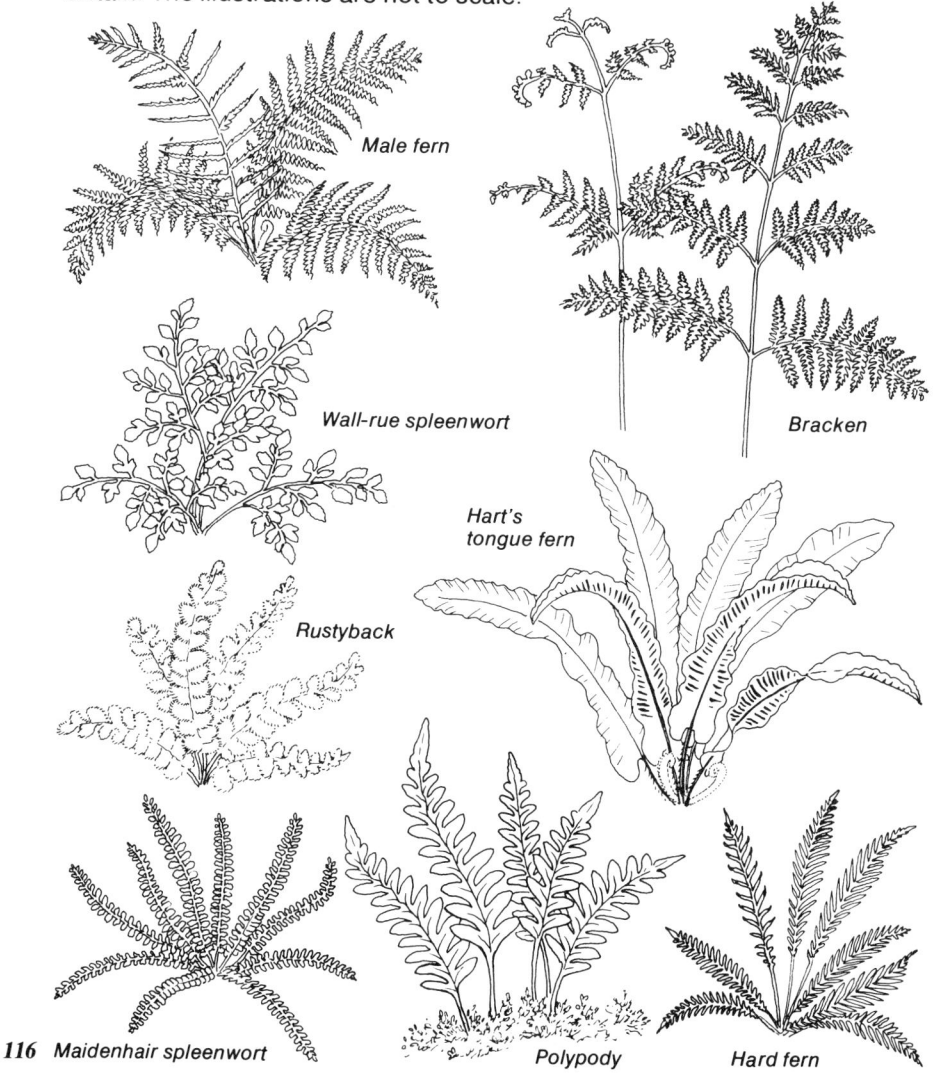

Male fern

Wall-rue spleenwort

Bracken

Hart's tongue fern

Rustyback

Maidenhair spleenwort

Polypody

Hard fern

TREES

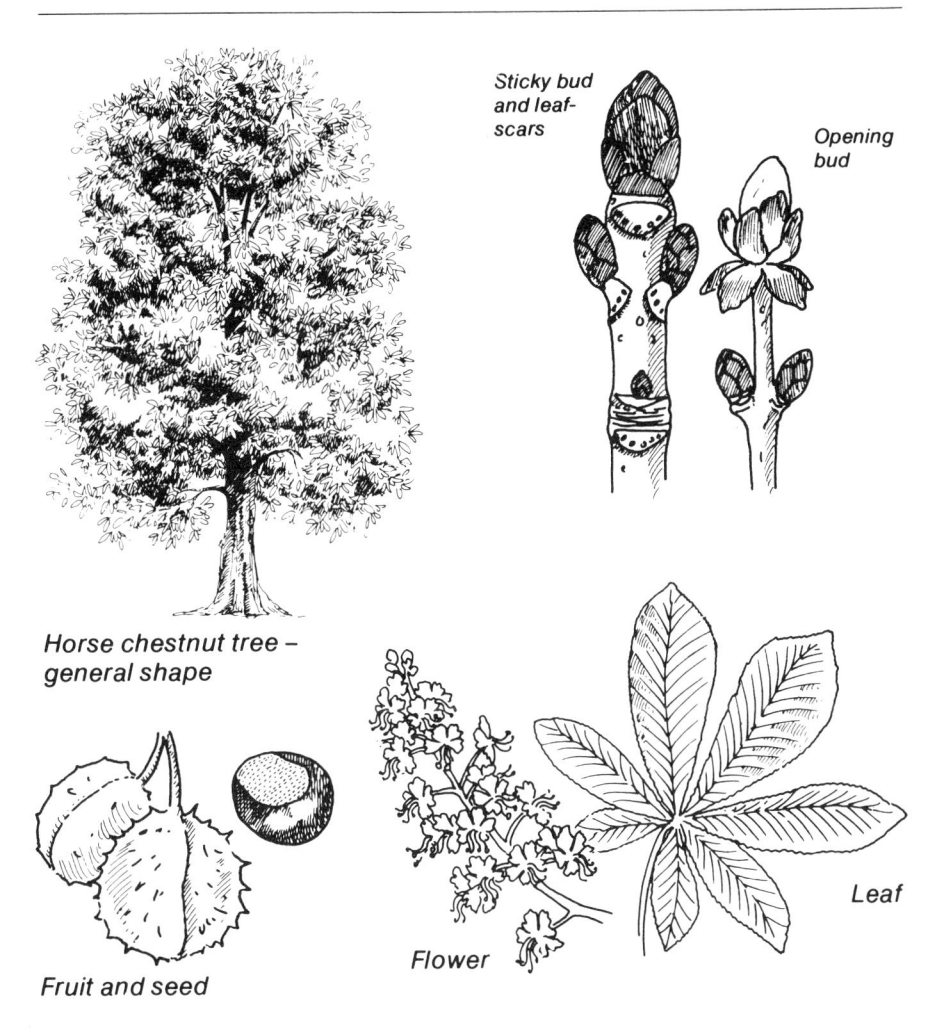

Sticky bud and leaf-scars

Opening bud

Horse chestnut tree – general shape

Leaf

Flower

Fruit and seed

General shape and branch shape: drooping, elbowed, etc.
Height: e.g. in relation to the average height of a telegraph pole.
Location: e.g. near or in woodland, etc.
Soil type
Bark: colour, texture, flaking, peeling, fissured, smooth, etc.
Leaves: colour, shape, size, veins, grouped or single, deciduous or evergreen.
Flowers: colour, shape, form, time of year.
Fruits or seeds: colour, shape, form, time of year.

MAMMALS

Apart from the occasional rabbit, it is unlikely that many mammals will appear unless the walker rises early and moves very quietly. On the other hand mammal tracks and signs may be seen. If an animal is seen, here are some tips to help with identification and to sort out some common mistakes.

Hare: large, gingery orange, generally solitary, fast runner.

Rabbit: smaller, grey with conspicuous tail, often in groups, lives in holes.

Rat: pointed snout, pink and hairless ears and tail.

Water vole: blunt snout, furry ears and tail, dives readily, aquatic habitat.

Mink: quite common and may be seen in daylight, dark chocolate-brown, smaller than a cat.

Shrew: very active, very small, long quivering pointed nose.

Vole: blunt nose, furry ears and tail, slower moving, very short tail.

Mouse: pointed nose, naked ears and tail which is very long, quick bouncing like a miniature kangaroo.

Stoat: larger than weasel – nearly 18 in. (46 cm.), black tip to tail.

Weasel: less than 10 in. (25 cm.), no noticeable black tip to tail.

FUR ON WIRE

Where animal paths lead under barbed-wire fences, tufts of hair caught on the barbs can often be found and thus the user of the path can be identified. Look for tracks as well.

Badger hair
– Coarse and black with white tips

Fox hair
– Soft and usually gingery-brown or black

HAZELNUT CLUES

Hazel can be found in the area covered by these walks, so it might be of interest to look out for any discarded hazel shells found near these trees. Small mammals have characteristic ways of opening the nuts and by examining the marks left on the shells the species of animal may be identified.

Bank vole

Showing only corrugated tooth marks around the edge of the hole and no markings on the shell surface.

Wood mouse

Showing tooth marks similar to those of the bank vole – around the inside of the hole but with markings on the shell surface as well.

Squirrel

Splits nut into halves along the seam, sometimes nipping the top off first. Young squirrels make quite a mess of a hazelnut shell when they are first learning the art.

SKULLS AND BONES

Surprisingly few skulls and bones are found in the countryside. Many dead creatures are eaten by scavengers, some of which, like the fox, also remove and hide this source of food. Others are buried by beetles or are covered with leaves or undergrowth. The diggings from badgers' setts are a good place to look as are discarded bottles and owl pellets. A hand-lens or magnifying glass may be needed to identify the smaller skulls. Skulls make interesting finds and can be readily identified using books on tracks and signs.

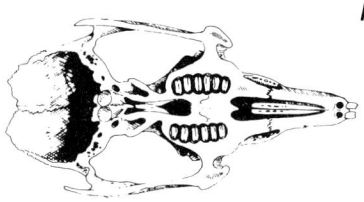

Rabbit skull

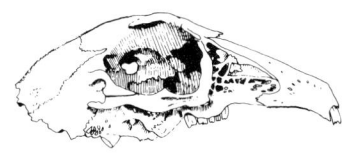

Underside of skull   Side view skull, lower jaw missing

ANIMAL TRACKS

The budding nature detective can learn a great deal from animal tracks. Firm mud is fine for recording tracks by using either plaster of paris or wax.

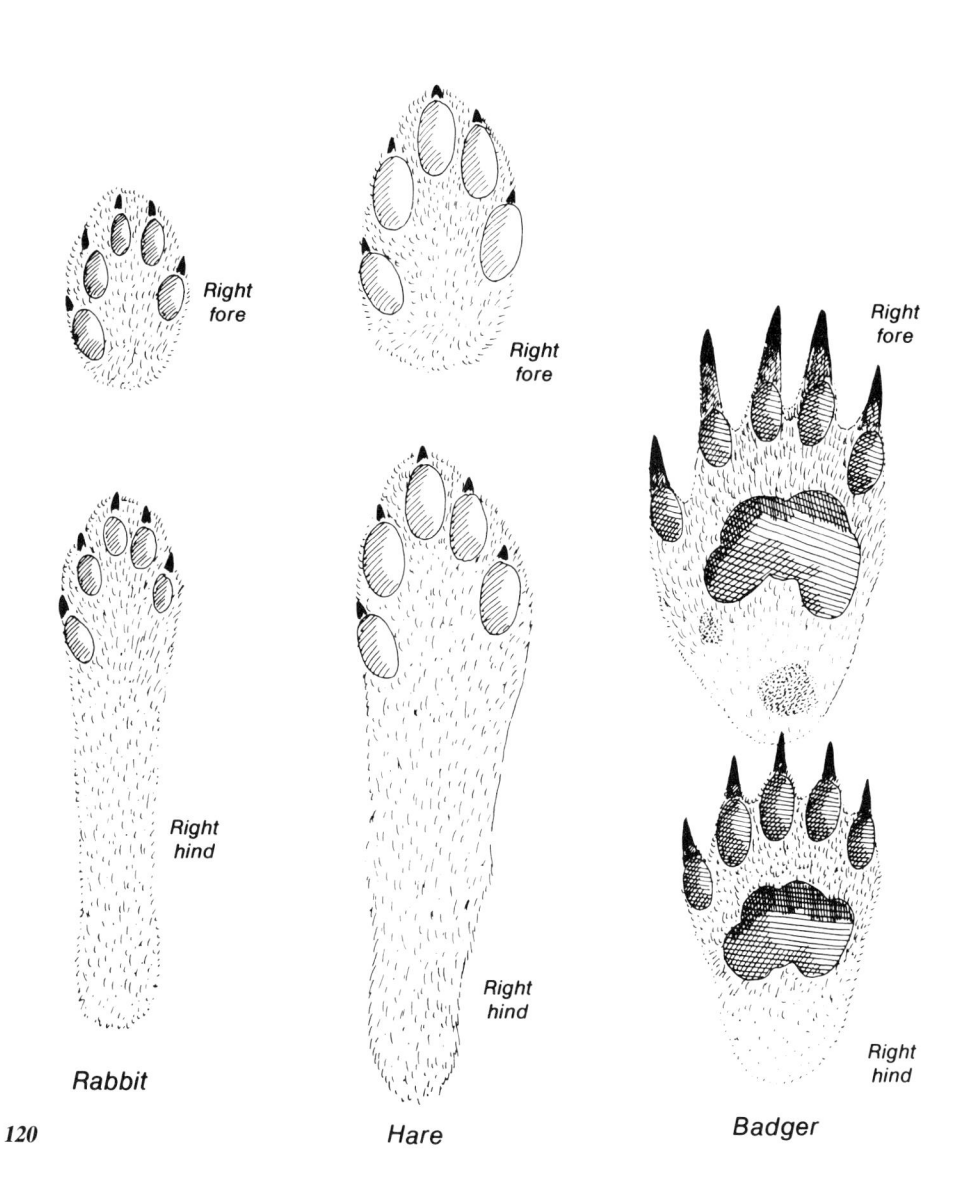

Right fore

Right fore

Right fore

Right hind

Right hind

Right hind

Rabbit

Hare

Badger

Squirrel

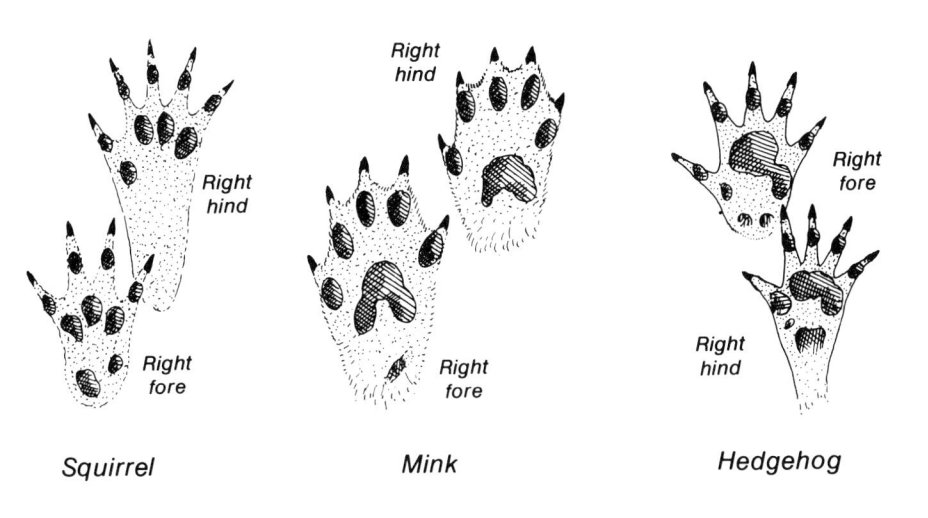

Mink

Hedgehog

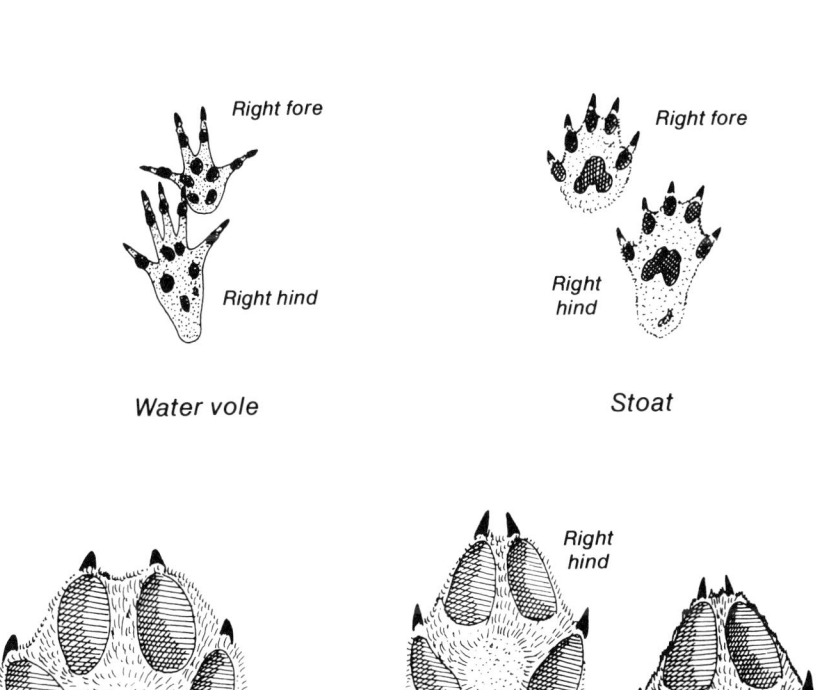

Water vole

Stoat

Dog

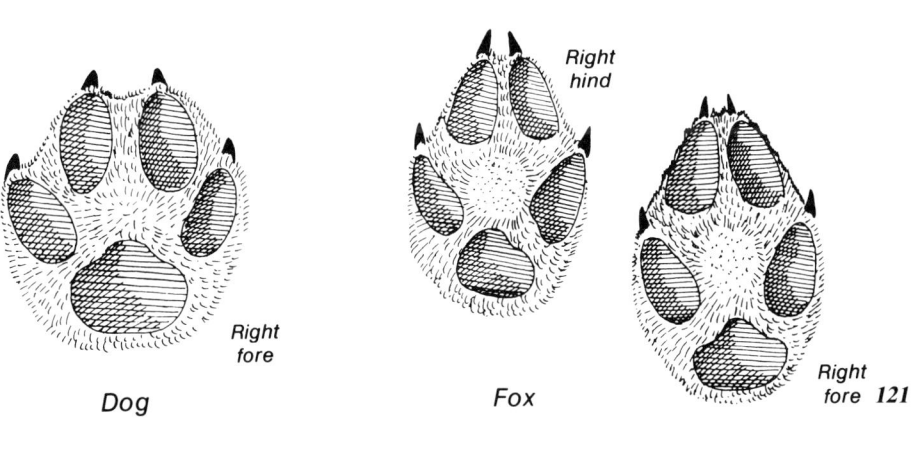

Fox

INSECTS and SPIDERS

GENERAL RULES OF CLASSIFICATION

Insects have:
 4 wings
 6 legs
 2 antennae
 three-part body

The insect class includes:
 beetles
 moths
 butterflies
 dragonflies and damselflies
 ants and aphids
 bees and wasps
 flies

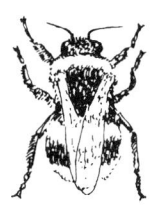

Bumble-bee

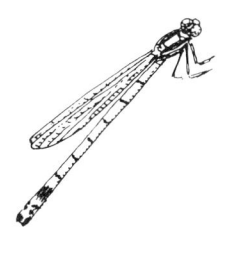

Damselfly

Dragonfly

Spiders have:
 no wings
 8 legs
 head and body

Spiders belong to a class called *arachnida*, including:
 harvestmen
 scorpions
 mites
 ticks

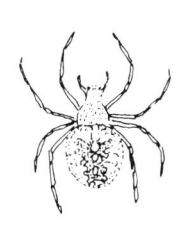

Common garden spider

WILDLIFE AND THE LAW

Under the 1981 Wildlife and Countryside Act, a large number of species gained protection. Set out below are some guidelines to the Act.

Plants:
It is illegal to take any part of some 62 plants and included in this list are many orchids. It is forbidden to dig up any wild plant unless the permission of the landowner has been obtained.

Reptiles and Amphibians:
It is illegal to catch, injure or kill:
    the Great Crested Newt   the Sand Lizard
    the Natterjack Toad   the Smooth Snake
and it is forbidden to offer for sale any other native reptiles and amphibians.

Mammals:
Some mammals, like the bat and the otter, are totally protected, therefore it is illegal to disturb them or even to damage their homes or prevent access to where they live. Other mammals, like the badger, have partial protection, which makes it illegal to kill or injure or to be in possession of a live or recently-killed badger.

Birds:
The law relating to birds is rather complex and if details are needed, the RSPB will help. Broadly speaking all wild birds, their eggs, and their occupied nests are protected by law from theft, disturbance, killing or taking. The exceptions are a few species which can be shot for sport or food, or are considered 'pests'.

If you cause no harm to wildlife and follow the Country Code, you should stay on the right side of the law!

LIST OF ORGANISATIONS

Urban Wildlife Group
131–133 Sherlock Street, Birmingham B5 6NB. Tel. 021 666 7474

Staffordshire Trust for Nature Conservation
Coutts House, Sandon, Staffs. Tel. 08897 534

Worcestershire Nature Conservation Trust
Hanbury Road, Droitwich, Worcs WR9 7DV. Tel. Droitwich 773031

Warwickshire Nature Conservation Trust
Montague Road, Warwick CV34 5LW. Tel. Warwick 496848

Bentley Emmanuel Wildlife Group
Church House, 13 Overdale Drive, Willenhall,
Wolverhampton, West Midlands. Tel. Willenhall 633867

Birmingham Natural History Society
26 Snowshill Drive, Cheswick Green, Solihull B90 4IJ. Tel. 021 728 3391

British Trust for Conservation Volunteers
Midland Regional Office, Firsby Road, Quinton,
Birmingham. Tel. 021 426 5588

Dudley Natural History Society
25 Dingle Close, Dudley, West Midlands. Tel. Dudley 50689

Pensnett Wildlife Group
77 High Street, Brierley Hill, West Midlands DY5 4RP. Tel. Cradley 71493

River Cole and Chinn Brook Conservation Group
Billesley Depot, Recreation and Community Services,
49 Poplar Road, Kings Heath, Birmingham B14 7AA. Tel. 021 444 3176

Royal Society for the Protection of Birds
Sandwell Valley Nature Centre, 20 Tanhouse Avenue,
Great Barr, Birmingham B43 5AG. Tel. 021 358 3013

Sandwell Valley Field Naturalists' Club
72 Dagger Lane, West Bromwich, West Midlands B71 4BS. Tel. 021 525 1143

Sutton Coldfield Natural History Society
71 Russell Bank Road, Sutton Coldfield B74 4RQ. Tel. 021 353 5044

Woodgate Valley Conservation Group
440 Ridgeacre Road West, Quinton, Birmingham. Tel. 021 422 6975

Yorks Wood Conservation Group
14 Yorkswood Drive, Kingshurst, Birmingham B37 6DU.

BIBLIOGRAPHY

Country Life Guide to Wildlife in Towns and Cities – Chinery and Teagle

Collins Guide to the Insects of Britain and Western Europe – Chinery

Collins Guide to the Grasses, Sedges, Rushes and Ferns of Britain and Northern Europe – Fitter, Fitter and Farrer

Collins Field Guides to:
  Freshwater Life – Fitter and Manuel
  Caterpillars of Butterflies and Moths in Britain and Europe
    – Carter and Hargreaves
  The Mammals of Britain and Europe – Van Den Brink

The Tree Key – Edlin (Warne)

The Wild Flowers of Britain and Northern Europe
  – Fitter, Fitter and Blamey (Collins)

The Mitchell Beazley Birdwatcher's Pocket Guide – Hayman

Discovering Hedgerows – Streeter and Richardson (BBC Publications)

The Unofficial Countryside – Mabey (Collins)

The Wild Side of Town – Baines (BBC Publications/Elm Tree Books)

The Mitchell Beazley Guide to Mushrooms and Toadstools – Pegler

Wildlife of the Sandwell Valley – Ed. Bloxham (SVFNC).

INDEX

Italic denotes illustration

Acacia, false (locust tree) 15
Adder (viper) 25
Aeshna, brown 55
Alder 17,18,53,73,76
Alder buckthorn 36
Alfalfa (Lucerne) 58,86,*86,*88, 89
Anemone, wood 76
Apple, crab 73
Arion slug *98*
Asbury, Thomas 19
Ash 35,53,57
Ash, mountain 53
Assassin bug 106
Avens, wood 28
Azolla 48

Badger 33,108
Balsam, Himalayan 83,84
Banded snail *90*
Bedstraw, marsh 80
Beech 19,20,26,33,53,*69,*107
Beech, copper 15
Beech mast *28*
Betjeman, John 15
Betony 73
Bibionid fly 83
Bilberry (whortleberry) 36,37, 96,*96*
Bilberry, hybrid 96
Bindweed *48,*49
Birch, silver 24,34,35,39,76,83
Blackbird 24,49,64,89
Blackthorn 23,56,73
Blocksidge, E. 30
Bluebell 23,*23,*65,76
Bogbean 34
Boletus edulis 35
Borage 85
Bracken 69,99,109
Bramble 56
Bright moth 29
Broome 97,104
Bryony, black 49,57
Bryony, white 48,*48,*49
Bullfinch 64,*64,*78
Bulrush, false (reedmace) 50, 99
Bumble-bee 49,53,69,84
Bunting, reed 17,49,50
Burnet, great 73
Burnet moth 106

Burnished brass 63
Butterbur 87
Buttercup 23,25,33,44,47,49, 79
Buttercup, celery-leaved 50
Butterwort, common 38,*39*

Caddis fly 78
Campion, red 49,83
Canada goose 18,54,*55*
Carp *16*
Celandine, lesser 47,76
Centaury, common 59
Chantarelle 34
Cherry, wild 73,76,78
Chestnut, horse 16,53,78,107
Chestnut, sweet 36
Chicory (succory) 54,*54*
Chiffchaff 25
Cinquefoil, marsh 55,99,100, *100*
Cinquefoil, yellow 99
Cladonia lichen 107
Clare, John 57
Cleavers 28
Clouded yellows 58
Clover, red 58
Clover, white 58
Cock's-foot grass 106
Colt's-foot 29,64,*64*
Comfrey 85
Contoneaster 18
Coot 17,18,48,54
Cormorant 94
Corn cockle 88
Cornflower
Cowberry 96
Cowslip 78,*79*
Cranberry 96
Cricket, water 88
Crowberry 96
Cuckoo 105
Cuckoo flower (lady's smock) 63,97
Cyclops 46
Cypress, swamp 15,16,17

Dabchick (little grebe) 43,48
Daisy, ox-eye 25
Daphnia 46,*46*
Darwin, Charles 96,100
Dead-nettle, white 49

Dogwood 36
Dove, collared 49
Drone fly 83
Druid's Well 37
Duckweed 65
Dunlin 17

Elder 20,25,49,57
Elm, English 35,57
Emperor moth 40,*40*

Feverfew 63
Figwort, common 54
Flag, yellow 24,55
Fly agaric 35
Fieldfare 64,*64*
Fox 14,108,*109*
Foxglove 54,88,109
Foxglove pug 63
Frog, common 25,45,46,65,*65,* 104

Gall mite 23
Garden (cross) spider 74,*75*
Garlic, hedge 56
Gentians, wild 59
Gipsywort 109
Golden rod 83
Goldeneye duck 18,94,*94,*95, 99
Goldfinch 77,*77*
Gorse 36,39,40,97
Grass of parnassus 63
Grass snake 25,26,*26*
Grasshopper 56,104,*104,*106
Graves, Robert 27
Great diving beetle 25
Greater celandine 47
Greater spearwort 16,*16*
Greater stitchwort 26,*28*
Grebe, great crested 16,17,18, 48,95,*95*
Greenshank 18
Grenville, R. H. 74
Groundsel 103
Gull, black-headed *13,*70,99
Gull, glaucous 94,99
Gull, great black-backed 99,*99*
Gull, herring 99
Gull, Iceland 94,99
Gull, lesser black-backed 99

126

Hairstreak, green 27,*27*
Hairstreak, purple 20,*20*,27
Harmon, John 33
Harvestman 85,*85*
Hawker, brown 55
Hawkweed, mouse-ear 25,86
Hawthorn 20,24,25,35,55,56, 57,64,76,106
Hay rattle 79
Hazel 57,73
Heather 40,*97,99,104*
Herb robert 63,83
Heron 34,39
Hogweed 28,56,58
Holly 20,33,34,35,*36*,66,69
Holly blue 36,*36*
Honeysuckle 30,47,*48*,49
Hop 87
Horsetail, common 67
Horsetail, wood 67,68,*68*
Hoverfly 25,83

Ichneumon wasp 83,*106*
Ivy 25,28,35,49,66,*66*
Ivy, ground 49

Jay 20,24,25

King cups 80
Kingfisher 49,*49*
Kipling, Rudyard 37
Kittiwakes 99
Knapweed 89,109

Laburnum 58
Lady's mantle 73
Lammas growth 89
Lapwing 39
Larch 36
Large skipper 63
Lewis, C. S. 90
Lime 53,54,*54*,59
Lime, large-leaved 53
Lime, small-leaved 53
Linnet 77,95
Liver fluke 100
Liverwort 38,*38*
Lousewort 39,63

Magpie 13,20,45,64,78
Male fern 83,*84*
Mallard 17,18,54,93
Maple, field 56,76
Marbled minor 63
Marsh fritillary 33
Martin, house 18,50,86,*86*
Mayfly nymph *47*
Mayweed, scentless 103

Meadow brown 16,58,63
Meadowsweet 80
Merlin 44,*44*
Milne, A. A. 33
Mink 29,*30*
Mint, water 50
Moorhen 54,105,*105*
Moschatel 76,*76*
Mugwort 45,56,86
Mulberry 53,59
Mulleins 54
Mussel, painter's 36,37,*37*
Mussel, swan 37
Mycorrhiza 45

Nature Conservancy Council 63
Nemephora degeerella 29
Nettle 86
Newt 46
Newt, smooth *46*
Nightshade, black 103
Nightshade, enchanter's (bittersweet) 29,*29*,56,106
Nightshade, woody 56,57
Noctule bat 18,*19*
Nuthatch 28,*28*

Oak 19,20,24,25,33,34,35,44, 55,57,64,69,76,89,107
Oak, cork 15
Oak gall 20
Oak, holm (evergreen) *14,15, 16*
Oak, Lucombe 15
Oak, red 36,53
Oak, sessile 53
Oak, Spanish 15
Oak tortrix 55
Oak, Turkey 15,53,78,107,*107*
Orange-tip 97
Orchid 39,45
Orchid, marsh 24
Orchid, Southern marsh 45,*46*
Osier 17,87
Oyster fungus 57,*57*
Oystercatcher 17

Pansy, field 103,*103*
Perfoliate St. John's wort 58, 88
Pheasant 20
Phytomyza fly 36
Pimpernel, bog 63
Pine 33
Pine, Corsican 36
Pipistrelle 18,59
Pipit, meadow 17
Plantains 44

Plot, Robert 29
Plover, ringed 17
Pochard 17,18
Pond skater 59
Poplar, grey 15
Poplar, lombardy 83
Poppy 47,103
Primrose 33

Queen Anne's lace (cow parsley) 49,70

Ragged-robin 39,80,*80*
Ragwort 77,88
Red admiral 58,89,*89*
Redpoll 95
Redshank 18
Redwing 64
Reedmace swamp 17
Rhododendron (tree rose) 15
Roach 59,*59*
Robin 64
Rose, dog 25
Rose, guelder 17,44,49,63,73, 78
Rose, wild 57,64
Rowan 33,35,36,44,76
Royal fern 67,*67*
Royal Society for the Protection of Birds (RSPB) 18,95
Ruddy duck 17,*17*
Ruff 18
Rush, sharp-flowered 74

Sainfoins 58
Sallow 87
Sandpiper, common 17
Scabious, devil's-bit 33,34,*34*, 80
Scabious, field 73,83,88,*88*
Scaup, little 94
Scorpionfly 59,60,*60*
Sedge, lesser pond 50
Shakespeare, William 25
Shelley, P. B. 94
Shepherd's purse 103
Siskin 95
Skylark 17,94
Small heath 58,97,*97*
Small skipper 58,97
Smooth snake 25
Sneezewort 39,73
Snipe 17,39,*39*
Sorrel, sheep's 25
Southern hawker (aeshna) 87, 87
Speckled wood 27,63

127

Squirrel, grey 14,16,45,59,*60*, 70
Snapdragon 54
Spangle, red 20
Sparrowhawk 70,77,*77*
Spearwort, lesser 33
Speedwell, germander 49
Sphagnum moss 63,66
Spindle 36
Spruce, Norway 53
Starling 20,44,98
Step, Edward 100
Stevenson, Robert Louis 44,104
Stickleback, three-spined 109, 110,*110*
Stitchwort 76
Stoat 80,108
Sulphur tuft 34,*34*
Sundew, round-leaved 63,100,*100*
Swallow 18,20,45,50
Swan, mute 18,93
Swan, whooper 17
Swift 50
Sycamore 57

Tabley, Lord de 107
Tansy 109,*109*
Tare, hairy 29
Teal 17

Teasel 77,88
Tench 59
Thistle, marsh 39,80
Thistle, spear 29
Thrush, mistle 49
Thrush, song 23,89
Timothy grass 106
Tit, blue 24
Tit, great 24,69
Toad 25,46
Tolkien, J. R. R. 63,65,70
Tormentil 39,80,99,100
Tortoiseshell 89
Tree creeper 26,28
Trefoil, yellow bird's-foot 58
Tu Fu 87
Tufted duck 17,94,95
Tufted hair-grass 75,*75*
Twite 95

Vetch, common 47
Vetch, purple tufted 58
Vetchling, meadow 58
Violets 33
Vole, water 50,*50*

Wagtail, pied 93,*93*
Warbler, willow 23,50
Water cricket 88
Water lily, fringed 34
Water rail 32,48

Water spider 47
Wayfaring tree 49
Weasel 79,80,108
Weld 103
Whirligig beetles 59
Wigeon 18
Willow 17,35,57,73,87
Willow carr 17
Willow, pussy 69
Willowherb, great 57
Willowherb, rosebay 29,58,74,83,84,104
Wisteria 58
Woodbine 49
Woodcock 33
Woodpecker, great spotted 70,*70*
Wood-pigeon 20,24,44,83
Wormwood 45,*45*
Woundwort, hedge 28,56
Wren 23,49

Yarrow 103
Yellow archangel 76,*76*
Yellow, clouded 89
Yellow, pale-clouded 89
Yellow-wort 59,*59*
Yew 16
Young, Andrew 50

128